WORKING WITH PURPOSE

FINDING A CORPORATE CALLING
FOR YOU AND YOUR BUSINESS

Jane Kise & David Stark

Augsburg Books
MINNEAPOLIS

WORKING WITH PURPOSE
Finding a Corporate Calling for You and Your Business

Large-quantity purchases or custom editions of this book are available at a discount from the publisher. For more information, contact the sales department at Augsburg Fortress, Publishers, 1-800-328-4648, or write to: Sales Director, Augsburg Fortress, Publishers, P. O. Box 1209, Minneapolis, MN 55440-1209.

Scripture passages, unless otherwise marked, are from the New Revised Standard Version of the Bible, copyright © 1946, 1952, 1971, 1989 by the Division of Christian Education of the National Council of the Churches of Christ in the USA. Used by permission.

Scripture passages marked (NLT) are taken from the Holy Bible, New Living Translation, copyright © 1996. Used by permission of Tyndale House Publishers, Inc., Wheaton, Illinois 60189. All rights reserved.

Scripture passages marked (NIV) are from the Holy Bible, New International Version, copyright © 1973, 1978, 1984 International Bible Society. Used by permission of Zondervan Publishing House. All rights reserved.

Library of Congress Cataloging-in-Publication Data
Kise, Jane A. G.
  Working with purpose : finding a corporate calling for you and your business / Jane A.G. Kise, David Stark.
    p. cm.
  Includes bibliographical references.
  ISBN 0-8066-5155-5 (alk. paper)
  1. Businesspeople—Religious life. 2. Business—Religious aspects—Christianity.
I. Stark, David, 1955- II. Title.
  BV4596.B8K53 2004
  248.8'8—dc22   2004008265

Cover design by Kevin van der Leek Design, Inc., and Laurie Ingram
Cover art from Getty Images/Stone
Book design by Michelle L. N. Cook

The paper used in this publication meets the minimum requirements of American National Standard for Information Sciences—Permanence of Paper for Printed Library Materials, ANSI Z329.48-1984. ⊖ ™

Manufactured in the U.S.A.

08   07   06   05   04   1   2   3   4   5   6   7   8   9   10

CONTENTS

ACKNOWLEDGMENTS

We could not have written this book without the assistance of friends and colleagues who willingly met with us, dialogued, and critiqued our ideas. Thank you especially to Ted Bailey, Ken Brown, Jim Dogan, Debbie Ducar, Lee Fratzke, Cathy Holte, Dave Janiszewski, Rose Larsen, Russ Lillienthal, Bill Maclean, Carl Moe, Derrick Moe, Jonathon Reckford, Pam Swensen, Mark Thompson, and Carol and Ron Vantine.

David thanks his grandfather, father, and mother, who kept alive the entrepreneurial spirit in the Stark family. Jane is ever grateful to the examples of Jim Dogan and Linda Gilligan, and the memory of Mike Leivian—three kindred spirits who modeled what it means to work with purpose.

CHAPTER 1

THE ALL-AMERICAN MYTH

*Myth: an ill-founded belief held uncritically, especially
by an interested group.*
  —Webster's New Collegiate Dictionary

A FRIEND OF OURS, MATT, GOT LOST AT HIS OFFICE ONE DAY.
Actually, he knew exactly where he was. He just had no idea
how he'd gotten there or, more importantly, *why* he was there.
Perhaps Matt's story isn't all that different from yours or from that
of someone you know.*

How did Matt get lost? It probably started when he was twenty
years old and decided to get his MBA—not a bad decision; Jane
holds an MBA as well. Matt figured his degree would be the ticket
to financial security, allowing for more leisure time.

By the time he graduated from a top business school, Matt was
twenty-five years old and married with a child on the way. When he
landed a job in the marketing department of a giant consumer
foods conglomeration, his classmates said, "What a perfect opportunity to show what you can do."

* Names and product details have been changed.

1

Matt soon got his chance. Within eighteen months of coming on board, he was assigned to the marketing campaign team for a new product: Cheesy Chomps Snack Chips. All the team had to do was create ads that made children demand their Cheesy Chomps while letting mothers know that these chips had as much calcium and vitamin D as a glass of milk. Other than the fat content, Cheesy Chomps were a perfect blend of junk food and health food.

Matt threw himself into the project, working sixty hours a week as the team pulled together focus groups of both adults and children to test their ideas. The project was exciting and the workload only temporary. One of his coworkers commented, "Really, what could be more thrilling this weekend than working on Cheesy Chomps?"

They launched the product during the back-to-school season. Matt and the rest of the team waited impatiently for the first sales indicators. What if the moms viewed Cheesy Chomps as just one more nutritional disaster? What if kids equated them with bran cereal?

A few weeks after the product launch, the corporate president called the whole team to his office. Matt walked slowly down the executive suite hallway, relishing the thick pile carpet and the artwork that adorned the oak-paneled walls. This was what hard work could bring!

The president handed each of them a copy of the quarter's sales reports and a glass of champagne, saying, "We're up 12 percent, thanks to Cheesy Chomps, the most successful new product in the history of this company. A toast to all of you!"

Matt joined in the back-pounding and congratulatory remarks, thinking, "This is success, this is what I'm working for."

But before sending them away, the president said one last thing: "Next year we need a sales increase of at least 13 percent. I know I can count on you to make upcoming new products as big as Cheesy Chomps!"

Matt felt the energy drain from his limbs as he walked toward the elevator. How could anyone work any harder than they had? And could profits continue to increase if it took such a giant success to do it? Funny, they had never talked about these things in business school.

THE MYTH THAT MUDDLES MATT'S THINKING

One cannot blame Matt for getting lost, for nearly all of us suffer from the same disorientation that washed over Matt as he left that gathering. We are enthralled by the most compelling myth in America today, one that subtly bombards us from dawn until dusk with its message. That myth is perhaps best represented by a woman we'll call the Mattress Lady. Perhaps you remember her from commercials a few years ago.

She wakes up, obviously well rested from sleeping on her special mattress—not a hair on her head is mussed. She glides downstairs in a stunning dressing gown, sets the table with china and glassware, and fixes bacon and eggs for her three children, who are clearly excited about heading to school.

As soon as she kisses the last one good-bye, she dons a power suit and leaves for the office. Chief executive of her company, the only female on the board, she presides over a meeting where all charts show the numbers going up, up, up. Then it's off to aerobics at 11 AM. She smiles through the whole workout.

Back to the office to take care of paperwork, then home by 2:30 to bake cookies for the children, which they munch happily as she helps them with homework. A college-age babysitter arrives, our lady slips into an evening gown while her husband adjusts his black-tie attire, and they drive to the opera in their Rolls Royce. They have time for a romantic moment by the fountain before returning for another restful night on their special mattress, the product being advertised.

Do you see the myth? According to the message, you have the wrong mattress—in fact the wrong car, job, babysitter, clothes, and even the wrong family. To be happy, you need to acquire what this family has: money, beauty, success, leisure time. Our entire consumer culture is based on this, the acquiring myth.

We're not advocating selling everything and joining the self-sufficiency movement. Instead, we're suggesting that we take a hard, long look at the motives behind our drive to work, to succeed, to acquire—beginning with how we got to where we are.

WHAT MADE US SWALLOW THIS MYTH?

Perhaps the myth began on July 4, 1776, when Thomas Jefferson penned the phrase, "We hold these truths to be self-evident, that all men are created equal, that they are endowed by their Creator with certain unalienable Rights, that among these are Life, Liberty, and the pursuit of Happiness."

Until that point, only a handful of people on earth had time to think about whether they were happy, let alone time to pursue happiness. Compare Jefferson's prose with these words being used at funerals during the same time period from *The Book of Common Prayer*: "Man, that is born of a woman, hath but a short time to live, and is full of misery. He cometh up, and is cut down, like a flower; he fleeth as it were a shadow, and never continuith in one stay" (Oxford: Oxford University Press, 1867, 243).

Considering that life might be happy was a radical thought; to *pursue* happiness was downright revolutionary. In many parts of the world it still is. Ask peasants in developing countries whether they are happy and their usual reply is, "I've never thought about it. I'm too busy trying to survive."

In the West, though, we've been taught that pursuing happiness is an *unalienable* right—it cannot be transferred, surrendered, or withdrawn. In the past two centuries, it's become reality for most Americans, due to incredible changes in several areas:

Health
With life expectancies for men climbing from 48.3 years in 1900 to 74.2 in 2000 (and from 46.3 to 79.9 for women), we have more healthy years to look forward to. When the Declaration of Independence was written, only about half of all children lived past the age of fifteen; now, dreaded stealers of children such as whooping cough and diphtheria are almost unheard of.

Vocation
Only in the past few decades have the majority of Americans had true choice in vocation. Before that, women who did not marry could be teachers, secretaries, or nurses. Men went into the same line of work as their fathers or joined the local industry, be it mining or farming or manufacturing. With mobility, universal education (in the 1920s only one in four teens received a high-school diploma), and new industries and career paths constantly appearing, most of us are free to pursue a variety of work choices.

Leisure

While rush-hour commuting and soccer schedules may seem to rob us of leisure time, we aren't hauling our clothes down to the river to scrub them, canning tomatoes to save our families from scurvy over the winter, or harvesting wheat with nothing but a scythe. We have time to pursue the things that make us happy.

People used to have a very different view of how to pursue happiness—and, if defined properly, it is part of God's plan for our lives. Jesus instructed his disciples, "I came that they may have life, and have it abundantly."[1] People used to be clear on where to find that abundant life, too:

> *O Lord of hosts, happy is everyone who trusts in you.*[2]

> *Happy are those who observe justice,*
> *who do righteousness at all times.*[3]

> *I know that there is nothing better for [workers] than to be happy*
> *and enjoy themselves as long as they live; moreover, it is God's gift*
> *that all should eat and drink and take pleasure in all their toil.*[4]

> *In the service of God man finds his true,*
> *though imperfect, happiness in this life.*[5]

So how did we get to where the Mattress Lady is our drive to work, to succeed, to acquire? In the beginning, it was subtle. When people had to first grow the flax, then spin the threads, then weave the cloth, then sew the garment, who wanted more than a couple of outfits? But when you could order from a favorite retail clothing catalog, who didn't want a few color choices in the closet?

Then came electricity instead of wood-burning stoves. Thank heavens! And the option of parlor music via the record player rather than listening to Cousin Francis whose twelve years of piano lessons did not exactly prepare her for the concert stage. And larger homes that stopped sibling warfare in shared bedrooms.

But now this country has more shopping malls than schools. The average American spends more time shopping than interacting with his or her children each week. A friend asked a little girl from the suburbs where she lived. "Ridgedale," she replied, which was the name of her mother's favorite shopping center.

Is the acquiring myth really making us happier?

THE MYTH UNMASKED

In a way, don't you wish the acquiring myth were true? We (Jane and David) would buy that mattress in an instant if it were. As it is, we have the teenagers, the power suits, and a knack for baking cookies. Get the mattress, trade in our movie tickets for the opera, and . . . we still wouldn't be like the Mattress Lady. Money can't buy happiness.

We need enough money for adequate food, clothing, shelter, and education—remember Maslow's Hierarchy of Needs? However, once we attain that basic level of security regarding our own survival, additional money doesn't make us happier.

Studies show that multimillionaire lottery winners are no happier a year after their lucky number is drawn than they were before collecting their winnings. Stories abound of estrangements from lifelong friends who don't think the winners are sharing the wealth nicely enough, of divorces, and of major regrets over how quickly the millions of dollars disappeared—spent perhaps on weddings that didn't last the year.

A survey of *Fortune* magazine's list of the wealthiest people showed that they were *less* happy than the average American. Perhaps this shows the fallacy of thinking that money can buy happiness—someone always has *more* than you.

Money . . . fame . . . success . . . leisure . . . all we need to do is look at the tabloid headlines to know that these things don't buy happiness. Tragically, humankind has known that truth for thousands of years. The author of Ecclesiastes experimented with the acquiring myth. He tells us that he built houses and reservoirs to water his gardens and groves, became the biggest livestock owner in Jerusalem, and built his treasury of silver and gold to rival that of royalty. Yet money didn't buy happiness for him:

> Those who love money will never have enough. How absurd to think that wealth brings true happiness! The more you have, the more people come to help you spend it. So what is the advantage

of wealth—except perhaps to watch it run through your fingers! People who work hard sleep well, whether they eat little or much. But the rich are always worrying and seldom get a good night's sleep.[6]

Perhaps you're thinking that you aren't under the spell of the acquiring myth. There are a few subtle variations that can be just as blinding:

I'm only trying to earn more to provide security for my family. What's wrong with that?
Nothing, but the vast majority of people never feel that they have enough; our targets for adequate income seem to increase with our income levels.

I'm only pretending to go along with the acquiring myth—just until I have enough. Then I'll leave the rat race behind and pursue my dreams.
In researching his book *What Should I Do with My Life?* Po Bronson found that financial independence didn't trigger life changes; something had to make the futility of the pursuit of money become personal. One investment banker quit his job after he returned from yet another trip and his toddler son didn't recognize him. For others it was divorce or illness. Still others faced reality only after being fired. For many people, shifting away from the acquiring myth borders on the impossible.

Once I'm successful, it'll be easier to pursue meaning and purpose.
Being steered by the acquiring myth fundamentally changes who we are. The values shifts are so fundamental that we aren't even interested in our old goals for meaning and purpose.

Further, many midlife crises are triggered by the absence of success—that sickening realization that you aren't going to become CEO or write a prize-winning play or win the U.S. Open. The depression that accompanies such realizations points out how much we're depending on success to bring happiness. Meaning and purpose are often lost.

Somewhere along the line, we confused pleasure and happiness; often, money can buy pleasure, but the effects are temporary. Teens learn that no one wears *that* brand of jeans anymore. The once state-of-the-art computer crashes every time you try to download something. Or perhaps you were the first on the block to have a home surround-sound theater, but then your neighbor installs digital surround sound . . . or a ceiling-to-floor plasma screen . . . or a second theater so that their children don't have to watch the same movies.

What's wrong with wanting to enjoy public television specials on a fifty-inch television or buying a boat for family outings or outfitting the kitchen with new pans and a food processor? Perhaps nothing, unless the acquiring myth keeps us from seeing reality, from seeking other goals that might bring true fulfillment. Thirty years ago, most college students considered family or living authentically as their most important goals. Now the majority say it's being well off financially.

Another ancient figure would like to speak to those students, a man we'll call the Rich Fool. Like the majority of Americans, the Rich Fool[7] decided to make his fortune and then retire. We aren't told whether this man inherited his fertile farmland, or whether he worked hard to procure his initial capitalization, but one year his harvest was so abundant that his storage facilities were soon overloaded. "I know what I'll do," he said. "I'll tear down my barns and build bigger ones. And, I'll store up all my grain and goods. Then I can relax for years—eat, drink, and be merry!"

The acquiring myth blinded the Rich Fool to a crucial reality: that life is finite. That very night he died. What if the Rich Fool had seen through the facade of the acquiring myth? Instead of being preoccupied with barn building, he might have considered the "big" questions of life: Who am I? Why am I here? What am I supposed to do with my life?

As long as we concentrate on what we don't have—money, status, youth, power, leisure time, and anything else we might yearn for—we aren't concentrating on what we can be, what we can create. Further, it's affecting more than just our individual lives; it's affecting our corporate existence, the corporate entity called humanity, because the acquiring myth is the fundamental driving force behind the most powerful institutions on Planet Earth: corporations.

THE ACQUIRING MYTH SYNDROME

As we wrote this book, a thick pall of disillusionment, disappointment, and déjà vu hung over corporate America's image. Enron, WorldCom, Tyco, CEOs, managers of mutual funds, auditors . . . the list of villains seemed to increase with each CNN broadcast.

Peter Carlson of the *Washington Post* perhaps gave voice to all of our feelings when he described *Business Ethics* as one of the world's thinnest magazines. While it is a thin magazine, it was begun with noble purposes in the 1980s when the savings and loan and junk bond scandals rocked the corporate world. Its founders saw themselves as watchdogs for corporate responsibility, handing out awards for environmentalism, social accountability, and employee ownership plans. Annually, they published a list of the 100 Best Companies to Work For in America. Enron was on that list.

Marjorie Kelly, editor of *Business Ethics,* wrote in the August 2002 issue about how Enron had fooled everyone at Corporate Social Responsibility (CSR): "It had great policies on climate change, human rights, and (yes indeed) anti-corruption. Its CEO gave speeches at ethics conferences and put together a statement of values emphasizing 'communication, respect, and integrity.'" But being fooled by Enron wasn't the real lesson. Instead she says, "The lesson is that all the things CSR has been measuring and fighting for and applauding may be colossally beside the point. Because they fail to tell us what's really going on inside companies."

What was really going on was the acquiring myth. Enron was built on it; the corporate culture teemed with multimillion-dollar Christmas parties and lavish executive perks. When informed about the accounting irregularities, Kenneth Lay, Enron's CEO, cashed in another $1.5 million in stock options and then looked into the pros and cons of firing the whistle-blower.

This is the natural course of events when the ticket to happiness is *acquiring* and success is measured by how much we *have.* Companies have to show ever-increasing results and market share to be considered successful—and those at the helm are given incentive packages to make sure that increasing that return on investment (ROI) is their goal.

TAKING OUR SHARE OF THE BLAME

This book isn't about thrashing corporate America. Most of us are dependent on corporations—for our livelihood, for medical care, for the food we eat, even for the books we want to read. The drive to succeed in corporate America has led to incredibly creative innovations that have improved our lives. Businesses aren't inherently bad. Further, businesses are made up of people and are dependent on people to purchase their stock, their products, and their services. A great many of us are just as guilty as corporate America of pursuing that acquiring myth. A friend of ours put it well:

> I bought a tech stock at $8. I could have sold it at $45, but I held on for more. I could have sold at $40 and been satisfied with a five-fold return on my investment, but I wasn't about to sell for less than its top value. I could have sold at $32, at $16, but I didn't . . . I was too greedy to recognize its true value. Now I can't even get $2 for it!

The acquiring myth keeps us from focusing on what is truly important: our corporate calling. The words of Martin Luther King Jr. challenge that myth to its very core: "I submit to you that if a man hasn't discovered something he will die for, he isn't fit to live." King was right; the person who dies with the most toys does not win.

ANOTHER DANGER

Besides its incipient ability to keep us from searching for what will truly make us happy, there is another fallacy inherent in the acquiring myth. If every corporation insists on increasing profits, if every country expects its economy to keep growing, if each of us wants a better house, a better car . . . what happens to a planet with finite resources? We have only so much land, air, water, minerals, and time. Infinite growth, as defined by the acquiring myth, is impossible on a finite planet. We can't all have more!

For a moment, forget the buildings and lawns and trees and rocks you usually view from your windows. Picture the earth as it looks from space. Try to recall, or imagine, the world's reaction in 1968 when those first pictures were beamed from *Apollo 8*, crystallizing as never before that our planet is a luminescent, breathtakingly beautiful bubble in the vastness of space. It's more imaginative and luxurious than any five-star resort or Hollywood set. And, it's home, our only home.

As people all over the globe stared at those images on Christmas Eve, 1968, astronauts Borman, Lovell, and Anders read from the opening chapters of Genesis, awed by the privilege of being the first to view our planet in this way: "In the beginning God created the heavens and the earth."[8] There were a few protests about reading the Bible on government time, but these quickly faded, overshadowed by the splendor and finiteness of our only possible home in space.

To really appreciate the impact of those pictures, though, think back on the rest of 1968. The war in Vietnam seemed to spin out of control. Both Martin Luther King Jr. and Bobby Kennedy were assassinated. That summer during the Chicago Democratic National Convention, over one hundred demonstrators ended up in local emergency rooms. Accusations of police brutality threatened to spark further riots. In October, presidential candidate George Wallace announced, "I think there are many times when it would be most efficient to use nuclear weapons. . . . I don't believe the world would end if we exploded a nuclear weapon."

Add riots on college campuses, the evening casualty reports from the war on the nightly news, and the world somehow seemed headed for catastrophe. No wonder people stared at those images from the crew of *Apollo 8*. Around the world, there was a new awareness that we had to learn to live on this earth together.

Sometimes it takes an entirely new view of things before we realize what is urgent, what is essential in our lives. In many ways, the year 2001 delivered the same kind of wake-up call as did 1968. In the aftermath of September 11, cries for rethinking our basic values as a country resounded from colleges, churches, legislatures, boardrooms, synagogues, high schools, even rock-concert arenas and football stadiums.

More cries resounded as the magnitude of corporate scandals surfaced. It's tempting to blame everything on greedy, power-hungry CEOs. And, it's tempting to clamor for new laws, new regulations, and more government oversight to stop such gross misdeeds. We all wanted to find ways to reclaim those multimillion-dollar salaries that the executives kept while employee retirement plans floundered—and take the perpetrators to trial and show them the insides of a jail cell.

Biblical wisdom—and experience—should tell us that such cries are misguided. Somehow, the lessons learned are lost and a new generation of insider traders or tax evaders takes the place of those who erred in the past. Experience shows that expecting threats of prison to deter these behaviors cripples people from evolving toward higher levels of morality. If there are too many rules or too great an emphasis on control from the outside, the inner development of being able to tell right from wrong is stifled.

In other words, we need a system that calls people to hold themselves to high standards—a corporate calling—not one that sets the standard for them. Understanding this concept is easier if one considers the development of biblical law.

Stage 1: The Letter of the Law

At this stage, rule-givers try to design laws that cover every contingency, believing that more rules will halt abuses. For example, God's law, "Remember the Sabbath Day and keep it holy" seems clear. Exodus 16:29 concisely stated, "Do not leave your place on the seventh day." But what was one's place? How far could one go?

Over the years, the priests and rabbis defined a Sabbath journey as two thousand cubits from one's home (whether the Hellenistic 1-foot, 6-inch cubit or the Roman 1-foot, 9-inch cubit was still debatable). Or you could plan ahead—have someone else carry one of your possessions two thousand cubits from your home, letting you go an extra two thousand cubits beyond that place. . . . The scribes were as ingenious as modern-day accountants in finding ways to journey as far as they wished.

While laws and regulations are necessary, "The Letter of the Law" breeds ingenuity, not responsibility. In fact, it shifts thinking from "Am I being moral?" to "Everything I'm doing is legal!"

This mentality led to Enron chief financial officer Jeffrey Skilling saying before Congress, "I was not aware of any inappropriate financial arrangements." In the wake of Enron and WorldCom, sweeping legislative changes were suggested; some were enacted. While more corporate oversight is necessary, "Letter of the Law" legislation hasn't worked to change corporate America. As long as the CEOs and the directors are guided by the acquiring myth, new laws simply intensify the search for loopholes.

Stage 2: The Golden Rule

The golden rule—"Do to others as you would have them do to you"[9]—is often held up as a universal moral standard full of wisdom and common sense. Further, most major religions have some version of it, making it seem useable in our politically correct environment.

Two problems arise. First, many executives don't "do to themselves" very nicely. We've seen firsthand how some executives interpret the golden rule as it applies to the Sabbath day of rest. "I don't ask anything of anyone that I won't do myself. If I'm in here seventy hours a week, there's no reason everyone else shouldn't work just as hard." Making the assumption that everyone is driven by the acquiring myth can overthrow the intent of the golden rule.

Second, interpretation of the golden rule often slips into "It's a dog-eat-dog world. I need to eat others as they would eat me. . . ." By itself, the golden rule isn't enough to overcome the power of the acquiring myth.

Stage 3: The Way of Christ

The third way, the Way of Christ, goes straight past rules to the heart of the matter, as illustrated by Jesus's approach to Sabbath laws. Matthew, Mark, and Luke all record instances where Jesus broke the laws of the Scribes on keeping the Sabbath. His reply to the scandalized Pharisees: "The Sabbath was made for humankind, and not humankind for the Sabbath."[10] The Sabbath was meant to give rest, not for debating how far someone could walk or whether it was better to starve than perform work by harvesting a bit of grain, as the Scribes had seen Jesus's disciples do.

Time and again, when people asked Jesus to interpret the letter of the law—or even the golden rule—he threw a higher principle back at them. Peter wanted to know if forgiving someone seven times was enough, but Jesus said, "How about seventy times seven?"[11]

Jesus tells us it isn't enough to follow the law. We need to understand the purpose of the law and abide by that higher principle.

We won't get rid of the acquiring myth through rules and regulations, nor through "universal principles" such as the golden rule, although those may be necessary stop-gap measures while we work toward fundamental change in the story that rules our lives. Something must take the place of the acquiring myth. That "something" is the truth of who we are and why we're here.

SUBSTITUTING REALITY FOR MYTH

To discover our true purpose, our corporate calling, let's go back to the beginning when God created the heavens and the earth. Think for a moment about our earthly home: We get to live in this phenomenal world filled with aardvarks and geysers and waves perfect for surfing and newborn babies and meteor showers. God created our earth, a place filled with so many wonders that those who are awake to them will never lack marvels to enjoy.

We're much more than guests of our Creator, though. The first few pages of the story of creation tell us that God placed us here to tend and care for the garden, the earth.[12] God has entrusted the earth to us. We are here to take care of it, to pass it on to the future. That's the first foundation of our corporate calling. Listen to how Jesus describes this view of why we're here:

> It's like a man going away: He leaves his house and puts his servants in charge, each with his assigned task, and tells the one at the door to keep watch. Therefore keep watch because you do not know when the owner of the house will come back— whether in the evening, or at midnight, or when the rooster crows, or at dawn. If he comes suddenly, do not let him find you sleeping. What I say to you, I say to everyone: "Watch!"[13]

That's our assignment. Individually and corporately, we are not here to acquire all that we can, but to tend to the place where we are privileged to live. We are *stewards* of the earth. A steward is someone who can be trusted to take care of things while the master is away. It's our corporate calling to watch over God's creation and to carry out what God needs done.

The choice is ours: to join in with God's plans or to ignore the impact of the acquiring myth on our children, our society, our work, and our planet.

As we've compared what God has to say about our corporate calling with the news events of the past few years, we believe that humankind cannot wait any longer to change its course. Why now? Think of the decision we face in terms of current headlines:

- Corporate failures
- Human rights violations
- Structural unemployment
- Growing class struggles, both nationally and internationally
- Terrorist attacks against centers of financial and military power

Are the current problems big enough? Or do we want to wait until they're even bigger before we topple our national myth? Which headlines will make us change? Another dozen Enrons? The death of the coral reefs? Constant terrorist attacks?

We can change those headlines if we change the myth. We can find our corporate calling and read about employees who trust their leaders. About businesses teaming together to protect the oceans. About corporations that made a significant difference in the quality of life of another country. We can face reality that we're called to be trustees of our earth.

THE NEED FOR CORPORATE, NOT JUST INDIVIDUAL, CALLING

Because work is such an enormous part of our lives, and because businesses hold so much influence over us, individual change will not be enough. In fact, what we do in the other arenas of our lives will scarcely matter if we do not also have an impact on corporations, for the largest multinationals have far more influence on political, environmental, social, and economic issues than any government. Corporations are now the most powerful organizations in the world. If you doubt this, consider what the acquiring myth has done to the following:

Our Sabbath day of rest. This has gradually disappeared so that consumers can acquire what they need seven days a week.

Our Laws. With states vying for corporate headquarter locations, companies influence everything from the tax code to environmental restrictions (or lack thereof). How much influence do they have?

Our Public Discourse. When the first edition of a book called *The Media Monopoly*[14] was published in 1983, fifty firms controlled most of the newspapers, magazines, television stations, and movie studios in the world. By the book's sixth edition in 2000, that number was down to six. The corporate interlocks are clearly seen in a quick glance at the major television networks: General Electric owns NBC; Disney owns ABC; Viacom owns CBS (as well as UPN, MTV, TNN, Nickelodeon, Paramount Pictures, Simon and Schuster, and other media companies). Corporate ties influence the news they provide to the public. So do their own economic needs. You might want to keep this particular ownership structure in mind if in reading this book you begin wondering why you haven't heard some of the information in these pages before.

Our Political Environment. In the 2000 federal elections, candidates and political parties received at least $60 million from the oil, gas, mining, electric, and automobile industries, all of which recommended that the Kyoto Protocol's mandatory reductions in greenhouse gas emissions be rejected. In contrast, environmental groups and alternative energy producers, groups with far less economic clout, gave $2.3 million. In 2001, President Bush rejected the Kyoto Protocol and committed to further study of climate change issues rather than action.

Note that the majority of Americans favored complying with the Kyoto Protocol and also consider protecting the environment as more important than economic growth. Who has the most power in this debate, citizens or corporations or government?

Economic Markets. Generally in economics, a global market is declared monopolistic if five firms control more than half of it. This is true in the markets for consumer durable goods, automobiles, airlines, aerospace, electronics, and steel.[15] And a preponderance of the big players are American corporations. We can't afford not to influence these global giants.

Another way to sum up the power of corporations is to compare their economic resources to those of governments. In *When Corporations Rule the World,* David C. Korton stated:

Of the world's hundred largest economies, fifty are economies internal to corporations . . . the world's 200 largest industrial corporations, which employ only one-third of one percent of the world's population, control 28.3 percent of the world's economic output . . . the global trend is clearly toward greater concentration of the control of markets and productive assets in the hands of a few firms. . . . [16]

Benjamin Barber, the author of *Jihad vs. McWorld,* describes how corporations are being allowed to define the world for themselves: "We call them multinational but they are more accurately understood as transnational or postnational or even antinational. For they abjure the very idea of nations or any other parochialism that limits them in time or space."[17]

If corporations are so powerful, then only one strategy is possible: If we wish to influence discourse and decision-making to break the power of the acquiring myth, we must influence corporations.

WHAT IS CORPORATE CALLING?

The best way to dispel a myth is to substitute truth for misconceptions. We need to replace the acquiring myth with a search for corporate calling, as embodied in five different areas:

Purpose

These are the corporate callings given to each organization and every individual. Instead of adopting the acquiring myth like the Rich Fool, some companies have the welfare of humanity in their vision. In *Built to Last,* one of the myths author Jim Collins shattered in his research on excellent companies is that they focus on maximizing profits. They don't. The best corporations have bigger visions than that.[18] Sunrise Senior Living, for example, starts with their vision: "To create senior living that champions the quality of life for all seniors." They emphasize choices in day-to-day living, service and care options, advocating for their residents as they negotiate the tangle of community, government, and nonprofit services that might help them meet their needs more fully.

Profits

Businesses are supposed to earn an appropriate return on investment (ROI), but part of our corporate calling is considering what would be an appropriate return on what we have been given. The Rich Fool couldn't think of anything to do with his profits but build bigger barns—an unproductive investment. He neglected to ask key questions such as, "Is my return honestly made? At whose expense? Is it sustainable over the long term? Is it appropriate, given the needs of other stakeholders?" While corporations must show profits to remain in business, how much is enough?

Products and Places

Corporations exist within societies, often within a multitude of different communities throughout the world. They have a choice of whether to look after just their own interests or to be concerned about the impact they have on communities. They can be Rich Fools, going for more at all costs, or they can consider the impact of who they are, the nature of their business, and the needs of those around them.

People

In acknowledging their corporate calling, businesses accept that they are responsible for the people who work for them. Companies can be Rich Fools, taking everything for themselves, or they can cultivate good relationships with their employees, allowing them to flourish in body, mind, and spirit, as well as provide a decent living.

Our Planet

Business leaders who embrace their corporate calling are also keenly aware that their assignment is temporary. Eventually they will hand over their responsibilities to the next generation. And, they will be judged by whether or not the vision can continue. Instead of Rich Fool tactics, depleting topsoil or ignoring the environmental impact of pesticides, they acknowledge the Native American proverb that "We do not inherit the earth from our ancestors; we borrow from our children." If one takes a long-term view, there are natural limits to what businesses can take.

On the one hand, these corporate callings may seem obvious. On the other hand, they go against a key principal of business, that the first responsibility of a company is to maximize shareholder profits. But true corporate calling and sound company policies can go hand in hand. In each chapter, we'll be giving examples of companies that have succeeded in melding business and calling—and have found that it's the only way to operate in today's environment.

WORK AND FAITH

Advocating for a corporate calling rather than the acquiring myth is different from insisting on religious values in the workplace. In the pages that follow, we hope to illustrate that following a corporate calling is sound business practice, no matter our religious beliefs. It just happens to grow from biblical wisdom.

However, there is another reason to set aside arguments about whether faith has any place in the business world. In *A Spiritual Audit of Corporate America,* Ian Mitroff points out that by building a wall around spirituality, declaring it off-limits in the workplace, we build up pressures around issues of the soul. He goes on, saying: "The worst thing about the wall, however, is that it is both an external and an internal division. It is external in that it walls off the organization from the deepest sources of creativity and productivity of its members. It is internal in that it produces a fundamental split in the souls of its members."[19]

We need to heal the division between our work and our souls. None of us can be true to our own corporate callings unless we are allowed to bring them into the workplace, acting to influence businesses to accept their responsibilities, their assignments, their own callings to work for the good of others.

Somehow, the church—another multinational organization— has to find its voice in this struggle for soul in the workplace, and we believe that what is good for the soul is also good for business, at least for businesses that want to exist for the long haul. The Matts of this world—and people who work for churches, governments, nonprofits, schools, healthcare firms, and mom-and-pop enterprises—all deserve a workplace that acknowledges their souls, their best source of creativity and productivity. Such a split in who we are doesn't have to happen. And it can't continue on this finite planet.

Corporate calling for business actually fits with the original posture of our country toward businesses. Toward the end of the 1700s, corporations didn't have a very good reputation in the Americas, for the best-known ones, such as the Hudson Bay Company and the East India Trading Company, were really extensions of the royal governments of Europe. They were given trade monopolies and the authority to make and enforce laws for the Crown. The fledgling United States had just escaped such tyranny and therefore set up laws so that corporate charters were to be granted by the state.

To incorporate, a business had to demonstrate some contribution to the common good. Until 1800, of the little over three hundred corporations in this country, only thirteen were chartered for manufacturing or commerce purposes. The rest provided some kind of public service ranging from building docks or canals to providing banking or insurance services.

But then, states started competing for businesses. In 1811, New York changed its laws so that businesses only provided a description of their intended enterprise to receive their charter. Other states followed suit over the next decades. Real power, though, came in 1886, when the Supreme Court ruled that a corporation was entitled to the same rights as a person under the Fourteenth Amendment of the Constitution: "nor shall any State deprive any person of life, liberty, or property, without due process of law." Companies used that ruling as leverage to overturn state laws covering working conditions and wage controls, and to declare any labor union activity as unconstitutional because it infringed on the rights of the corporation.

Since then, in the name of free enterprise we have allowed corporations to become more and more powerful. Every decade or so, a new scandal breaks out and we rush to pass antitrust laws, new reporting requirements, and so forth, but our politicians and economists continue to say that market forces are the best corrective. After almost two hundred years of granting more and more rights to corporations, perhaps it's time to rethink, as did the founders of this country, the fundamental role corporations should play.

We're living in a world of Rich Fools when it only makes sense to live out our corporate calling. Our goal is to give you a spiritual view of work that belongs outside of church, right in the workplace.

Anyone in business can use its language, uphold its principles, base decisions on its premises, and argue using its images, without proselytizing or apologizing. That spiritual view might look something like this:

Date: *Now*
To: *The Business Community of the World*
From: *God*
Re: *Stewardship of the Earth*

The events of the past couple of years illuminate the fact that this world is far from perfect. These events even blinded some from the fundamental reality that the world belongs to me. I'm well aware that this message is going out to many who don't believe that I exist, but I've spent most of history speaking to similar audiences. Let's not debate who, what, or where I am, but instead look for things we can agree on.

My plan for the earth is, and always has been, working. Giving humanity the ability to make choices about right and wrong was the toughest decision I made, for I knew that some would choose wrongly. But I wanted all of you to accept freely the assignments I created you to fulfill; anything less than free choice would make you my puppets, not cocreators of history.

While my work will be completed in the fullness of time, this is the season for your work. I clearly laid out your roles. Whether you work alone or with others, through communities or corporations, your calling right now is to feed the hungry, heal the sick, bind up the broken-hearted, set the captives free, strengthen the weak, house the homeless, and bring justice, beauty, reconciliation, and joy to communities all over the globe. Your privilege is to enjoy the world; your responsibility is to care for it on my behalf.

If you choose to embrace this assignment, be forewarned that systems, structures, and people may work against bringing out the best in yourselves and your dreams for others. Often, you'll find the same resistance within yourselves as you struggle with human flaws while striving toward my calling.

Concentrate on what I have given you: talents, gifts, abilities, motivations, and convictions to invest in productive work in this world. If the task seems too big, remember that I can do far more than you can ask or even imagine, by the power at work within you and within the world. I am giving you this world to hold in trust for me. This is your calling.
God

CHAPTER 2

CAN ONE PERSON
MAKE ANY DIFFERENCE?

I went to the woods because I wished to live deliberately,
to front only the essential facts of life,
and see if I could not learn what it had to teach,
and not, when I came to die, discover that I had not lived.
I did not wish to live what was not life, living it is so dear;
nor did I wish to practice resignation, unless it was quite necessary.
—Henry David Thoreau, *Walden*

IN 1845, HENRY DAVID THOREAU HEADED TO THE SHORES OF Walden Pond to escape from the troubles and anxieties of "modern life." Then twenty-eight years old, he had run a successful private school for a few years, but he sought solitude to determine what really mattered in life.

Similarly, Matt, whose story this book began, sought time for reflection after the Cheesy Chomps celebration, wondering if what he was living was really a life. If Thoreau's quest sounds too impractical to take to heart, compare it to how Matt's goal might have read before his Cheesy Chomps encounter:

I went to the corporation because I wished to live well,
to front only the material facts of life,
and see if I could not earn what it had to dole out,
and not, when I came to die, discover that I had not prospered.
I did not wish to own what was less, ownership is so dear;
nor did I wish to practice simplicity, unless I failed
to make six figures.

Matt's original choice was the natural one for people living under the influence of the acquiring myth. His Cheesy Chomps epiphany saved him from the subtle trap of *careerism*, a phenomenon so rampant that *Webster's Dictionary* carries a definition for it: "practice of advancing one's career often at the cost of one's integrity."

Like Thoreau, Matt wanted to find lasting purpose, the reality of our corporate calling, the truth about how we are to live. Thoreau spent two years and two months living by the shore of Walden Pond, pondering questions about meaning and purpose in the midst of a society growing ever more materialistic. That was over a hundred and fifty years ago, yet his thoughts remain valid. Am I really living? Or am I resigned to life as it is?

THE CORPORATE HERO'S QUEST

We can create Walden Pond moments for ourselves, setting out on a mission to discover what is lacking in our lives. Matt did so after the Cheesy Chomps celebration and realized that he'd bought into the acquiring myth, marking his path toward success and fulfillment against its measuring system. He decided to hunt for a position at another firm that would let him pursue a true calling. But as he searched, he discovered the pervasiveness of the myth; he knew he needed help if he was going to escape its grip. He started meeting with other sales and marketing people who were also young parents to discuss how they could gain control of their lives. At that point, Matt embarked on a classic hero's quest, as described by Joseph Campbell: "The usual hero adventure begins with someone from whom something has been taken, or who feels there's something lacking in the normal experiences available or permitted to the members of his society."[1]

Classic quest tales tell of destroying a terrifying enemy, overcoming danger and frightful trials to find true love, or seeking an object or wisdom that will end the threat to a town or city. Matt pursued his quest within the hallways of corporations. What made it a hero's quest was his desire to help others as well as himself. Joseph Campbell maintained that those who quest for selfish reasons were at best celebrities: "The ultimate aim of the quest must be neither release nor ecstasy for oneself, but the wisdom and the power to serve others."[2]

Scanning the headlines for examples of corporate greed, environmental problems, global inequities, human rights—the churning troubles that the acquiring myth has produced—can lead to yearning for heroes who are up to tasks that resemble the Twelve Labors of Hercules. However, if more of us admit that there's "something lacking in the normal experiences" of business and embark on a quest for the wisdom to influence change, what might happen?

Cynthia Cooper's quest began with a need to prove the value of internal accounting. "I loved it," she said of working at WorldCom. "We were moving and shaking and acquiring companies."[3] Cooper was in charge of budget standards and performance evaluations, while the financial statements were handled by external auditors.

But when another executive called her to report that $400 million had been taken from his reserve account, Cooper started making inquiries. The external auditors told her that it wasn't a problem. She grew suspicious. WorldCom's chief financial officer angrily told her to back off. Her team joined in the heroic quest of redoing the external firm's audit. And they found misclassifications of billions of dollars of operating costs that artificially boosted earnings. The final figure by which profits were inflated totaled $9 billion, the largest accounting fraud in history.

Along with Sherron Watkins of Enron and Coleen Rowley of the FBI, Cooper was named as *Time* magazine's Persons of the Year for 2002. All three at first refused the honor; they were just doing their jobs. But they were surrounded by people who could have taken the same kinds of actions—and didn't. Only these three had the courage to embark on the lonely journey of the hero.

As you try to envision a society powered by corporate calling rather than the acquiring myth, remember that Thoreau moved back into the mainstream of life. Cooper, Watkins, and Rowley all made a difference right where they were. Debunking the acquiring myth doesn't mean leaving work behind, but instead finding ways to base your life on a better image and then joining the quest.

THE POWER OF ONE

Corporations are made up of people. We can't say that corporations are to blame for the pervasiveness of the acquiring myth because it blinds us to the fact that real people are behind corporate actions—and we each have a role to play, big or small, in changing the course of corporate power.

We also can't wait for heroes to appear; it wastes time. Most heroes are no different from us, but they prepared themselves to act. Each of us can do the same. Rosa Parks, for example, didn't simply decide to stay seated one day on a public bus in Montgomery, Alabama. For years, she'd been the executive secretary of the city's NAACP, but taking a stand for civil rights seemed impossible, living as she did in the heart of the South. Then she attended a workshop at Miles Horton's Highlander School. Miles trained community leaders to work for social change, drawing on their own resources rather than looking for solutions from experts. Of the workshop, Rosa said, "I found out for the first time in my adult life that this could be a unified society, that there was such a thing as people of different races and backgrounds meeting together in workshops, and living together in peace and harmony. It was a place I was very reluctant to leave. I gained there the strength to persevere in my work for freedom, not just for blacks, but for all oppressed people."[4]

In other words, the workshop helped Rosa Parks envision a future—and that vision gave her the courage to stay seated that day on the bus. Her act was not prearranged, but it came out of her work (she knew that her organization was looking for a legal test case; the bus law was unjust) and her vision (someone had to begin). The workshop jump-started her hero's quest. And her quest fueled quests for hundreds, then thousands of others in the Civil Rights Movement.

Claiming your corporate calling is a hero's quest you can join. To begin, consider whether the acquiring myth is the ruling story line of your life. What makes you get up in the morning? Where do the extra hours of your day go? How do you complete the sentence "My life would be happy if only . . ."

Once you've determined how large of a role the myth plays in your own life, it's time to act. You know that the acquiring myth is keeping people from finding true meaning and purpose in life, so you set out to do what you can.

One starting place is our LifeKeys[5] process, either on your own or through a seminar, to discover the intersection between what you do best and what God needs done in this world. Through LifeKeys, you can identify the gifts and talents you'd love to put to use for the causes that fill you with enthusiasm. That's your corporate calling, your responsibility toward the corporate body of humankind. Part of that calling may be through individual efforts, but part may be to influence the place where you work.

As you strive to embrace your corporate calling, pressures will no doubt mount from all sides to maintain the status quo, especially if the acquiring myth permeates your company. To determine the myth's influence, check the annual reports, the mission statement, and strategic plans—is the emphasis on growth in income and market share? (Another good measure is to count the number of cars in the parking lot that cost more than a teacher's or nurse's or retail store manager's annual salary.)

If you feel pressured by your corporate culture to uphold the acquiring myth, you have at least three choices:

1. *Quit your job and search for a better place.* Sometimes this is the best answer—your company's mission is so far removed from your own that in good conscience you can no longer work there. However, chances are that the same problems will pop up elsewhere, even at nonprofit organizations. Often, nonprofits are expected to service more and more people or provide an ever-increasing array of services in up-to-date facilities under the premise that if a program is good, bigger is better.

2. *Stay and ignore the dissonance between the company's actions and a better corporate calling.* Sometimes this seems the only answer, especially if you are the sole wage earner in your family or the job market is especially tight. However, there's a fine line between playing it safe and selling your soul. Thoreau called it practicing resignation. Ask yourself, "Ten years from now, will I be glad that I stayed?"

3. *Work from inside to change things.* Sometimes staying put is the best way to be the best steward of what you have.

The last alternative may sound absolutely impossible—you are too far down in the chain of command to change anything—but it isn't. In the chapters that follow are "top-down solutions" regarding each of the five callings for leaders and managers, laying out a new vision of business and some practical guidelines for change. After each of those sections are "bottom-up strategies" which contain ways for you to answer your calling in your own life, ways to make a difference at work, and thoughts on persuading others to join in the effort.

CHOOSING TO WORK FOR CORPORATE CALLING

The point isn't how big of a role we can play but how well we play the role we've been given. Choosing to stay may not be right for you and certainly won't be easy, but the following thoughts might motivate you.

Corporations Must Change

Weighing the magnitude of corporate influence is overwhelming. In fact, it's tempting for anyone not in a position of power at a company to say, "There's nothing I can do—I can't win against corporate America." However, our choice is clear: We can continue to declare ourselves helpless or we can find ways to remind corporations of their calling to operate in the public interest.

Again, corporations are made up of people. And people, not corporations, set policies, learn, change, take risks, dream dreams, and envision the future. In *Deep Change*, Robert Quinn writes,

> Though we often prefer to believe that nothing can be done about the awful problems we face, there comes a time when we have to take on the system because the system needs to change. There comes a time when we need to "just do it."
>
> When we do decide to initiate action, there are no written guarantees, no insurance policies that will save us if we fail. . . . Leaders cope with this presence because they understand that whenever they sacrifice their principles for pressure, both they and the system take another step toward slow death.[6]

In some way, shape, or measure, we all have a corporate calling. Refusing that assignment may seem like playing it safe, but in truth it is deadly. The result is either a life void of meaning or one filled with regret at the chances ignored and the dreams left unexplored.

If Not You, Then Who?

We're hoping you see that there's really only one choice to be made:

> If we each have a corporate calling,
> and our individual assignments tie in with humankind,
> then there must be something for each of us to do
> to work toward substituting the vision of corporate calling
> for the acquiring myth.

The call to change the world may sound reactionary . . . or repetitive . . . or too radical. If you're thinking that much of what went on in the 1960s was also a backlash against the acquiring myth, you are in part correct. However, there are two crucial differences between what happened then and what we are suggesting.

First, the crisis wasn't nearly so great. Corporations weren't so powerful, the United States still seemed a safe haven from the rest of the world, and the world's population was just over three billion. It's now over six billion.

Second, the movements then succeeded at pointing out what was wrong with our society, but they didn't propose a solid alternative. To declare the acquiring myth just that, a myth that is leading us away from what is truly important, it must be replaced with an even bigger vision: corporate calling. And the efforts of people at all levels will be needed for that to become a reality.

Further, some of the biggest battles in history have been won through the efforts of a few people who said, "Things can't continue the way they are . . ." and shaped a new vision. The Civil Rights Movement, Solidarity, the end of Apartheid, the end of a dictatorship in Romania—the way to make corporate calling a reality is to act.

OKAY, BUT HOW?

In his book *The Answer to How Is Yes*,[7] consultant Peter Block points out that whenever people face seemingly impossible tasks, the most frequent question is, "How? How are we going to pull this off?" However, when we are facing essential issues of life and death for those who live on this planet, the only possible answer is, "Yes, we are going to do this."

Not how? But "yes." As we said "yes" to reaching the moon. As we said "yes" to one person, one vote. As we said "yes" to providing education to every child in this country. According to Block, the wrong questions put the following blocks on our problem solving:

- "How do you do it?" rushes past the question of whether you've found the right question and looks. to others for answers.
- "How long?" points to speedy answers rather than commitment to deep change.
- "How much?" monetizes values, ignores other costs, and puts people at risk.
- "How do you get people to change?" suggests controlling others rather than admitting our own roles in the world we create.
- "How do you measure it?" makes things that can be measured the test of success and ignores meaning and purpose.
- "How have other people done it?" gives way to a life of imitation rather than affirming trust in creativity when we work with others.

Saying "yes" can force us to step outside our comfort zones, but as Block points out, "Most of us do not think of ourselves as radicals fighting oppression. The oppression that we might consider, however, are those things around us that do not support the values we care most about."[8]

Throughout this book we will be pointing out what individuals can do, even those not in a position of power, to change our society's ruling image from acquiring to one of corporate calling. While we will be discussing biblical principles, in every case what the Bible tells us about business and the current research on best practices in business coincide. Again, you won't have to proselytize or apologize if you say "yes" and start working toward a new image for the business of business.

A NEW IMAGE

As you ponder the new image we are proposing for business, consider as well the image you carry of yourself. On your daily commute to work, do you feel like a drone or worker bee, a nameless face in a corporate crowd? Or are you a cog in the office machine, easily replaceable if you don't fit or if you break down? Or are you straight-jacketed in a position where systemic problems or power struggles keep you from having the influence you hoped for?

To get to a new image, set aside the amount of influence your job description says you have and think of your bigger purpose in life. Tell yourself, "I'm on assignment—my corporate calling. This happens to be my current job. How can I use my job to fulfill my corporate calling?"

Then, choose a new image of how you will do that. Anyone in business, from the CEO to the mail delivery staff, can choose to prod those around them toward the reality of their corporate calling by taking on a new view of what is possible. Here are some image ideas:

- *An earthworm.* Before you dismiss the lowly status of the earthworm, consider its assignment—to tunnel underground, out of sight, aerating the soil and allowing other things to grow. Perhaps you prefer to influence by affirming other people or by creating environments where they can flourish.
- *A watch dog.* Well-trained dogs are friendly toward those they try to protect and hostile to threatening beings. Perhaps you prefer to influence by searching for threats to the true calling of business and warning those around you, taking action when necessary.
- *A sheep dog.* Border collies and others work to keep the herd together, away from dangers. Perhaps you can influence by keeping others within the boundaries of corporate calling and away from the acquiring myth.
- *A beaver.* Beaver dams are not built randomly; each stick is chosen for its spot based on thickness, length, and strength. Do you have the same ability to help people see their perfect role in a company? Perhaps you can influence by getting others to where they can have the most influence toward a new vision of business.

• *A honeybee.* When a bee finds a treasure trove of flowers, it returns to the hive and dances for the other bees, communicating the location of the nectar. Perhaps you can act like a bee, pointing toward new, life-giving directions for your team's goals, relationships, or vision.

Or make up your own image. Think of something that seems small, perhaps insignificant, yet can have a major influence. Even if you can't imagine yourself having an influence on more than a handful of other people, picture your efforts as planting a mustard seed. Remember the image?

> The Kingdom of Heaven is like a mustard seed planted in a field. It is the smallest of all seeds, but it becomes the largest of garden plants and grows into a tree where birds can come and find shelter in its branches.[9]

What if we each planted a seed, creating food and shelter and shade to block out the acquiring myth? Those who flourish will influence a few more, and those will influence more to do what is right, and a new image for business could become a reality, an end to the soul-stifling effects of power and greed and hubris.

Again, each of us has a choice to make. Think of the headlines you wish to read ten or fifteen years from now. Whether we choose to act or choose to do nothing, that choice will shape what they become. What do you want them to be?

What headline could your workplace be a part of? Dream about it, consider it, ponder it as you think about how your assignment fits within a vision of corporate calling.

It's time to choose . . . or the choice may just be made for us.

I believe that if you just do your little bit without thinking of the bigness of what you stand against, if you turn to the enlargement of your own capacities, just that in itself creates new potential.
    —Vandana Shiva, India, founder of Navdanya,
        an organization that strives to preserve agricultural diversity

CHAPTER 3

PURPOSE

Becoming What We Hope to See

You see things; and you say "Why?"
But I dream things that never were; and I say "Why not?"
—George Bernard Shaw[1]

TUESDAY MORNING, TEN O'CLOCK. TIME FOR THE WEEKLY senior management meeting. You've taken your usual chair in the executive conference room, close to the windows yet with a good view of the whiteboard. Thinking back, you remember that you've already had two cups of coffee, one at home and one during a quick read of *The Wall Street Journal* when you got to the office, so you reach for a bottle of water and a glass.

First on the agenda is a report from the head of the research department. She clears her throat a bit nervously as she pushes a few keys on her laptop computer to open her PowerPoint presentation. "This is an update on our inquiry regarding the drug Enactrozin," she begins as the first slide flashes on the screen. "Approved by the FDA just two years ago, it already accounts for over 12 percent of our income.

"But . . ." she pauses for a moment, "as you know there are reports that in as many as fourteen to twenty cases a year, side effects have caused death in users. That's well within acceptable safety limits in treating such a serious disease. However, our competitor has developed a similar drug that appears to have no side effects at all."

"Can we reformulate our product in a similar manner?" you ask.

"Not without repeating the FDA approval process," the presenter replies as another slide fills the screen. "This is our timeline estimate for returning an enhanced product to the market."

Silence fills the room as you and the other executives do a quick calculation on the bottom-line impact of withdrawing Enactrozin from the market. What will you decide to do?

This scenario was given to fifty-seven groups of executives and business students who were asked to act as imaginary boards of directors faced with such a decision.[2] Would they continue marketing such a drug, even though they knew a better alternative existed? Over 80 percent said, "Yes, we would keep selling it, and we'd take legal and political action to keep it from being banned. Our responsibility is to the bottom line."

Yet when the same researcher presented the same scenario to individuals, students, faculty, and business managers, more than 97 percent said that withdrawing the drug would be the socially responsible choice. Individuals said "no," while in a corporate setting similar people answered, "Go for the money."

Examples like this show how the acquiring myth can supercede the executives' beliefs about right and wrong. Where the acquiring myth sets the vision for a corporation, personal values vanish.

Can vision be that crucial? Merck, the pharmaceutical corporation, operates from several values, including, "We are dedicated to the highest level of scientific excellence and commit our research to improving human and animal health and the quality of life" and "We expect profits, but only from work that satisfies customer needs and benefits humanity."

In the 1980s, Merck developed a drug to cure "river blindness," a parasitic disease found in developing countries. They also partnered with agencies overseas for distributing the drug to a million customers who couldn't afford it. Employees at Merck know their corporate calling: improving life. Management understood that "failure to go forward with the product could have demoralized Merck scientists . . ."[3]

While not everyone will agree with all of Merck's efforts, the company tries to live out its vision and values. They offer two AIDS drugs at no-profit prices to sixty of the least-developed countries. In addition, Merck and the Bill & Melinda Gates Foundation each gave $50 million to the government of Botswana to partner together in supporting that country's strategy against the disease. While some groups criticize them for not doing more, Merck is actively doing more than drug research by working to create these kinds of partnerships to continue their corporate calling of making drugs available to all who need them. Their vision includes more than the bottom line.

MAKING MEANING OUT OF MISSION STATEMENTS

In Merck's case, their mission has true meaning to employees. Creating visions and missions for corporations goes in and out of fashion. For years, only directors or top management teams worked on visions, often while sequestered for long retreats away from the realities of business.

Complaints against those processes were twofold: either the statements had no connection with reality or they were so vague that they could have applied to any kind of business, from a campground to a computer manufacturer.

But missions do matter. For one reason, companies are made up of people, and people need meaning and purpose. If we abandon the acquiring myth as the chief source of motivation, the void it leaves needs to be filled with something more substantive.

The second reason is that companies become what they envision. Remember the *Muppet Movie* villain Doc Hopper, who wanted Kermit to be the "spokes-frog" for his chain of fried frog's legs restaurants? He espouses the vision, "All my life, I wanted to own a thousand frog's legs restaurants and you're the key, Greenie."

Kermit shudders, envisioning millions of frogs on tiny crutches, and says, "I have a dream, too. But it's about singing and dancing and making people happy. That's the kind of dream that gets better the more people you share it with."

Jim Henson was the voice of Kermit the Frog. And the mission of the Jim Henson Company is "to make the world a better place by inspiring people to celebrate life." One of Henson's employees said that if Henson said, "Let's make a show that will help children work for world peace," his associates would agree to try because Henson always accomplished what he set out to do—like finding a way for Kermit, a puppet, to ride a bicycle.

The world was shocked when Henson died of pneumonia at the age of fifty-three. We all wanted more of his celebration of life, and that's perhaps the biggest indicator that his company lived up to the mission he set for it.

There's a basic Doc Hopper verses Kermit the Frog choice to be made, and it starts with the core idea of the business. With a corporate calling, the purpose of your company is bigger than the products made or the services provided. The vision sets the tone for the organizational environment, actually defining what employees think they can and can't do.

Johnson & Johnson, for example, proudly touts its company credo, originally developed by General Robert Wood Johnson. The General Johnson presided over Johnson & Johnson as it grew into a world-class corporation. He believed that companies had a responsibility not only to shareholders, but to customers, employees, and the community. This became part of the company's credo in 1943, which begins:

> We believe our first responsibility is to the doctors, nurses and patients, to mothers and fathers and all others who use our products and services.
>
> In meeting their needs everything we do must be of high quality.[4]

Johnson & Johnson's Web site points out that "Putting customers first, and stockholders last, was a refreshing approach to the management of a business. But it should be noted that [General] Johnson was a practical minded businessman. He believed that by putting the customer first the business would be well served, and it was."[5]

Think back to Johnson & Johnson's actions in the wake of the Tylenol tampering tragedy. This credo guided the 1982 decision to pull all Tylenol from store shelves, even though only a few bottles in one location had been sabotaged with cyanide. The cost to shareholders didn't matter as much as the responsibility to customers. The employees of 1982 willingly acted on the vision of the credo they'd been given.

Johnson & Johnson isn't perfect; all of the companies we use as examples are made up of people and therefore stumble in one way or another. The company's handling of the Tylenol tampering, however, shows that at a basic level, they understand that within their mission of making pharmaceuticals lies the greater responsibility of caring for human life. They're aware of their bigger purpose, their corporate calling.

Envisioning a corporate calling rather than growth and profits doesn't mean settling for less. Instead, it means listening for a bigger vision than you might entertain on your own.

The recent self-help theme of envisioning yourself reaching your goals in order to attain them isn't new; it reaches back almost as far as written language. What *is* new, perhaps, is what we're told to envision. Victory? Wealth? Happiness? Marriage? Our ideal weight?

It's true that you might not reach your goals without a clear vision of what they look like and what it means to attain them. However, if you have the wrong vision, getting there may be the worst thing that can happen to you. So, how do you find the right vision?

"ASSIGNMENT" FUNDAMENTALS

The difference between ordinary mission statements and a corporate calling is the difference between a company that makes movies and the Jim Henson Company's life-giving vision of making the world a better place by inspiring people to celebrate life. That's their calling, the way they care for the garden, the earth God has given us.

If the Rich Fool represents the acquiring myth, then another ancient character known as "The Faithful Manager" is our model for finding our corporate calling, our purpose. To put the story in modern-day terms, the Faithful Manager worked for an investment firm. One day, the CEO called in three of his portfolio managers and said, "I'm taking a well-deserved extended leave and I know I can trust you to manage our investments while I'm gone."

The CEO knew who had the most experience and distributed the responsibilities accordingly. One manager was to oversee five investment areas; another, two; and the last only had to monitor one.

When the CEO returned several months later, the first manager handed him a financial statement and said, "See, I've doubled the value of your portfolio."

After checking the numbers, the CEO said, "Congratulations! Well done, my faithful manager. You've just earned a promotion. Your strategies show that you understand my intentions."

The second manager had also earned a significant return on his investments and was promoted as well. However, the third manager handed the CEO an envelope and said, "I knew you were a tough boss, so I converted the money to cash to protect the principle."

The CEO stared at this last manager in disbelief. "Cash? Even a T-Bill or a money market account would have provided interest, you fool!" With that, the CEO handed the cash to the first manager and a pink slip to the last.[6]

In essence, our assignment is to do the best we can with what we have been given to carry out our corporate calling. Put yourself into the story as a manager at a company run for God. As you try to determine your calling, consider the following:

- *The CEO trusted the managers to handle investments in his absence.* They were acting as his stewards, actively directing his affairs until he returned. He didn't spend time explaining what he wanted done with the money because he assumed they already knew their assignment: Invest the money as he would.
- *The assignments were given according to ability.* The managers all received different assignments. They weren't judged in comparison to what the others did, but in relation to what they were asked to do.
- *When the CEO returned, the managers gave everything back.* If you're on assignment, then profits go toward what God

wants done. Sometimes this means growing the business, but sometimes God has other plans.

• *The last manager misunderstood his assignment.* He was so fearful of doing the wrong thing that he did nothing. In truth, God wants us to do the best with what we have, not become paralyzed with fear that our best efforts won't be good enough.

What is true for individuals is true for corporations. They just may become what they envision—like the executives who could only envision profits and therefore would choose to continue marketing a defective drug. The drive for success blinds them to everything else they could accomplish. The difference between a true corporate calling and mere profit can be as striking as the difference between the life cycles of a mangrove swamp and a rain forest.

A RAIN FOREST VIEW OF CORPORATE VISION[7]

The charm of a mangrove swamp is in the knots, tangles, and every-which-way chaos of the plants that thrive along the salty, tidally inundated shores of coastlines. Special adaptations allow mangrove trees to excrete salt through their leaves, absorb oxygen through root extensions, and produce seeds that take root easily, allowing rapid proliferation of mangroves in areas that are hospitable to few other plants.

As the mangroves begin to flourish, their decaying leaves and roots create an environment where other plants and animals can grow. Birds, crocodiles, fish, and other plants are attracted to this nutrient-rich yet sheltering environment. Further, the denseness of the mango roots prevents shoreline erosion and filters run-off sediments, protecting nearby coral reefs.

However, a mangrove swamp isn't a very good place for a mangrove tree. As the cycle of growth and decay repeats, building rich soil around the mangrove's roots, eventually it is cut off from the water it needs for nourishment. It destroys its own ecological niche by rapid growth, proliferating so much that it has no place to go.

What does a mangrove tree corporation look like? How do they damage or destroy themselves? Note that the companies mentioned below are admirable in many ways, but consider whether another vision might have avoided the problems they faced:

- *By being too aggressive.* Think of how small towns are now fighting to keep Wal-Mart out—and seventy have been successful. Is Wal-Mart's retail vision universal or better suited to certain locations?
- *By being too controlling.* Think of Microsoft's battle with the justice department because of how it bundled its products. Could a different vision have served them better?
- *By assuming that phenomenal growth can be sustained.* Think of the glut of Beanie Babies. What if Ty, Inc. had included in its vision some thoughts about how many of the little things parents would truly want in a child's room?
- *By thinking that customers share their vision.* Remember the failure of New Coke?

Note that the one thing all of these possibly unbalanced visions have in common is a quest for growth. A "mangrove" vision can keep us from questioning our view of reality as we aim toward our goals.

We only have to look a few miles inland to find a new model for corporate vision: the rain forest. Teeming with an incredible variety of plant and animal species, the colors and sounds are the fiber of fairy tales. Viewed from the air, the phenomenal density of its tree canopy leads one to believe that rain forests must thrive in the richest soil on earth. But that isn't true. The soil is thin with very few minerals. Further, the lush canopy blocks sunlight from reaching the ground, inhibiting significant undergrowth. One can navigate the spacious floor of the rain forest easily.

Within this hostile environment, however, an incredible balance exists. Plants and animals adapt to fill niches. Like mangroves, many of the plants and animals inadvertently contribute to making the environment hospitable to other species. For example, leaves that fall to the ground are quickly set upon by insects, fungus, mushrooms, and other living things that nourish themselves while working to return the leaves' stored energy to the thin topsoil. Unlike the mangrove, each species stays within sustainable limits, maintaining their niches in the forest rather than overrunning those of other species.

Rain forest companies may not always be as newsworthy as mangrove companies—without rapid growth or spikes in earnings, they may not attract attention. How do they flourish?

By Finding a Worthy Niche

For example, Sally Fox, founder of Natural Cotton Colours, was appalled by the heavy use of pesticides in cotton production. She developed pest-resistant strains that produced brown, green, khaki, and auburn fibers, eliminating the chemical-intensive dying process as well. Her cotton is used by companies such as Fieldcrest and many specialty clothing stores.

By Aspiring to Noble Purpose

Mike Jenzeh left real estate brokering to somehow give what he could to someone else. While in Costa Rica, he visited a leather shop where workers handcrafted beautiful luggage and duffel bags. With the goal of helping those workers receive a fair return on their work, Mike founded Joseph Company to market the bags in the United States. He used Isaiah 58:11 as his personal vision: "If you spend yourselves in behalf of the hungry and satisfy the needs of the oppressed, then your light will rise in the darkness . . ."[8]

By Focusing on One Class of Customers

Edward D. Jones, a brokerage firm, says, "We focus on one type of customer: those interested in relatively high-quality, low-risk investments held for the long term."[9] To keep this focus, they avoid other clients that might interfere with the needs of its core customer base.

Edward D. Jones doesn't peddle its own set of mutual funds. They won't let their clients do Internet trading. And, they avoid almost all dealings with corporations and thus cannot be influenced by the high fees corporate clients can generate. For example, the firm was the first to downgrade General Electric's stock back in November of 2000—it didn't do any business for the huge firm, so, unlike many other brokers, didn't have to worry about repercussions from GE. Without such encumbrances, brokers at Edward D. Jones are able to give unbiased advice to their customers. And in both 2001 and 2002, it was listed first on *Fortune Magazine's* list of the 100 best companies to work for.

By Concentrating on Excellence Rather Than Growth
This is a mindset that trades short-term results for long-term success. Arie De Geus, a top executive at Royal Dutch Shell, warns, "[I]nstead of evolution, we go for revolution. Instead of building an enterprise, we set out on a quick adventure. We take a gamble. But good businesspeople are not gamblers. They should be the opposite; they are stewards and custodians of the company they manage."[10]

Note that all of these are big concepts that have to do with the actual design of a company—what it will be rather than what it will do. When Jim Collins and Jerry Porras conducted their research for *Built to Last*, they found that only three of the nineteen enduring companies they profiled had started with a great product or service idea. Instead, at companies like 3M and IBM and Citicorp, the environment for great ideas was developed first. The products came from outstanding structures, not the other way around.[11]

Those environments start with an overarching corporate calling that allows for rain forest rather than mangrove-style prosperity.

CORPORATE CALLINGS OF RAIN FOREST QUALITY

The following examples are just a sampling of the many kinds of missions that are paths to a corporate calling. The ways corporations interpret their callings stretch from those who believe that their only mission is to make money to those who literally want to change the world. In between are many worthy purposes.

A Mission of Spirit
Some companies truly live up to their missions. For example, Southwest Airlines based its mission on defining a niche and developing an excellence. Southwest Airlines doesn't offer many frills: no first class, no meals, no seat assignments. Instead, customers get low fares, consistent timeliness, and a feeling that they're not really on a commercial airline. Southwest's mission is "dedication to the highest quality of Customer Service delivered with a sense of warmth, friendliness, individual pride, and Company Spirit."

The warmth comes through in safety announcements such as: "If you haven't been in an automobile since 1965, the proper way to fasten your seat belt is to slide the flat end into the buckle. . . . As the song goes, there might be fifty ways to leave your lover, but there are only six ways to leave this aircraft. . . ."[12]

You might be on one of three Southwest planes painted like Shamu the Killer Whale—or on Lone Star One, painted like the Texas flag. To Southwest, warm and friendly customer service means having fun. Are your passengers stuck in long lines because of a weather delay? Offer a gift certificate to the one with the biggest hole in his or her sock. Stuck on the tarmac with a mechanical glitch? Hold a trivia contest. And for heaven's sake, if you want your employees to be fun-loving and enthusiastic, let them wear tennis shoes and polo shirts instead of high heels and suit coats.

More importantly, Southwest's mission led them to the industry's best records for being on time, handling baggage, and receiving the fewest customer complaints. The mission directs employees to be creative in delivering customer service—and it works. They were recently listed as the top-performing stock of the last thirty years by *Money* magazine.[13]

How do having fun and delivering customer service connect with a true corporate calling? Because customers are people. When people arrive at a destination with smiles on their faces they're less likely to succumb to road rage in the airport parking lot. Remember, we aren't judged according to the size of our assignments, but by the way in which we carry out the one we've been given.

A Mission of Giving Back

Leonard Lindquist, one of the founding partners of the Minneapolis law firm Lindquist & Vennum, infused the company's culture with his belief that out of gratitude for what their profession has given them, the partners need to give back to the community. Now in his nineties, Mr. Lindquist still mentors people in prison and raises money for various causes. At law firm gatherings, he speaks about the difference each person can make by helping those less well off, giving recognition to attorneys for their pro bono work or community leadership efforts.

Several years ago, the firm committed to meeting the American Bar Association's challenge to dedicate 3 percent of its billable hours to pro bono work. In 2001, the law firm devoted almost nine thousand hours to pro bono projects directed primarily to low-income persons and not-for-profit and other community organizations. Lindquist & Vennum is one of only a handful of law firms in the country where 100 percent of its attorneys participate. An example of their work was a ten-year effort on behalf of Albert Burrell, a Louisiana inmate who was developmentally disabled and had been sentenced to death. The firm staffed the court battle for a decade after finding compelling evidence that the man was innocent. At the end of this ten-year effort, Albert Burrell was released from prison, a free man.

A Mission of Providing

David Janiszewski realized his purpose at the seventieth anniversary celebration of the company his grandfather started in 1923. David watched his dad speak to over five hundred people—employees and their families—and noticed tears in his eyes. He asked his father, "What's it like to lead?"

His dad replied, "It's overwhelming. Three generations have worked for us. We're putting their kids through college; they're able to buy homes."

David knew that he, too, wanted to develop a successful business that provides security for his employees. In 1996, he started Convenience Learning International, an innovative e-learning company that creates interactive, video-intensive training materials. To him, being profitable means providing for his employees. He says, "I want to watch my employees succeed. As they buy homes and have children, it says to me that I'm giving them enough confidence in our ability to stay around for them to take risks. They believe in our purpose. That's a lot of responsibility to undertake. In a way it increases the pressure I feel to succeed, but it's my goal." If the company is ever sold, David has plans to allocate some of the proceeds to the employees and to donate much of the rest to charities.[14]

A Mission That Weds Responsibility and Profitability

WorldWise, Inc., enthusiastically states that its mission is nothing less than to change the world. Aaron Lamstein, its founder, knew he wanted to market environmentally responsible products. He started by finding niche products, offering to distribute them, and seeing what appealed to larger markets. Then the company began developing its own products, concentrating on pet and gardening supplies.

In other words, WorldWise started with a big mission and went searching for products and markets to fulfill that mission. They adhere to the following statement:

> Our contribution to the global goal is to provide useful everyday products that sustain both our customers and the Earth, and to educate consumers about sustainable living. Our product selections are rooted in nature. We evaluate the entire lifecycle of products for sustainability, from the harvesting of resources to recycling it back into the system.[15]

With distribution through seven thousand stores nationwide, including channels like Target and Home Depot, they've managed to become profitable as well as responsible. "The philosophy was, and continues to be: If we can offer a product that works as well or better, looks as nice or finer, and costs the same or less than a product that doesn't take as much consideration of the planet, who wouldn't make the environmentally responsible choice?"[16]

Again, the company has a corporate calling: being environmentally responsible and modeling how it can be done. Their Web site, www.worldwise.com, is full of tips for consumers who want to pursue sustainable living.

A Mission of Fairness

Sustainable Harvest works to encourage production of top quality coffees "in a manner that is socially just, environmentally sensitive, and economically viable. Our way of doing business ensures that the lands and families that produce our exemplary coffees will thrive for generations to come."[17] The founder, Daniel Grossman, worked to provide a guaranteed fixed price for growers that reflected their costs rather than watching them be put out of business by the commoditization of coffee. He believed that consumers would be willing to pay for organic coffee beans and he was right; so-called fair trade coffees are available in nearly ten thousand stores and institutional accounts in the United States. Sales in 2001 doubled over year 2000 sales.

This corporate calling of including more than your shareholders as your stakeholders is not only a fairer way to count the true cost of business, but is becoming more necessary in a media-linked world where inequities are increasingly transparent.

A Mission of Limited Growth

Patagonia, the outdoor clothing and equipment firm, has as its purpose, "to use business to inspire and implement solutions to the environmental crisis."[18] The company grows at a slower rate than the rest of the apparel industry, according to director of sourcing Roger McDivitt, rather than risk losing sight of their true purpose. "So far," he says, "the company has chosen to stick to its own design and environmental precepts, even at the risk of losing some sales for the moment. We'll say we're going after 7 percent growth and we think that's a big deal. And we know that, for many apparel companies, that's insufficient. But it's kept us in business for 30 years and I expect that we'll be around for the next 30 years."[19]

A Mission of Shared Wealth

Andersen Windows grew out of Andersen Lumber Company. The vision of mass-produced windows, novel in 1903, was shared by Hans and Sarah Andersen. Hans pledged that Andersen Lumber Company would always be "different and better." Herbert and Fred, their sons, continued that pledge.

Hans started Andersen Windows' employee profit-sharing program back in 1909. They were also early providers of such benefits as paid vacations, disability insurance, and savings incentives. On the product front, this company produced the first casement windows and wooden sliding doors, innovations we take for granted today. They began working on energy-efficient design features back in the 1940s, decades ahead of widespread demand. Their Perma-Shield products eliminated the need for storm windows.

In 1975, Anderson turned partial ownership of the firm over to its employees through a stock ownership trust financed 100 percent by the company. This ongoing commitment to sharing profits with employees can be linked to the corporate mission statement which values committed, productive, and talented working partners, as well as a stable workforce. As Fred Andersen put it, "A company is known by the values it keeps. . . . Enthusiasm, loyalty and pride of workmanship are qualities on which the reputation of our company depends. . . . It is the partnerships between all of us that makes it possible for us to be our best. . . ."[20]

LARGER-THAN-LIFE MISSIONS
Note the characteristics of the above missions:

- They are all much bigger than profit, even though the founders make a point that "higher purposes" can't supersede sound business practices. In other words, these businesses have substituted a corporate calling for the acquiring myth.
- They all use the language of business. Bigger spiritual values may be encompassed in the visions, and founders and employees are passionate about those visions, but the words bridge the spiritual and the business worlds.
- The focus is higher than industry or product. That makes them more long-range and universal.

In the 1990s an oil company conducted a study of companies that had survived for generations. Their motivation? They are fully aware that there may be no such thing as the oil business in a hundred years or so. Either oil reserves will be depleted or we will have developed new fuels to replace oil and gas. The oil industry is already looking for a way to evolve.

Their research showed that long-term companies did not define themselves in terms of products or industries (what they *did*). Instead, they defined themselves in terms of who they *were* and the purpose they had in the world. "Success for the company meant evolving into the best possible thing it could be and, in the process, to be good at what it happens to be doing in order to survive."[21]

Medtronic, Inc., for example, has as part of its mission "To contribute to human welfare by application of biomedical engineering in the research, design, manufacture, and sale of instruments or appliances that alleviate pain, restore health, and extend life."[22] This drives a corporate culture where every employee knows they aren't just working at a manufacturing firm; they're saving lives.

A few years ago, Medtronic considered dropping their line of drug pumps, which only accounted for $10 million in business. But Bill George, who was CEO at that time, knew their mission, "to restore health and life." They kept the program, thinking of all the diseases they could address, such as cerebral palsy. The pumps are now their fastest-growing line, thanks to a company vision that was bigger than just implant devices. With that kind of corporate calling, Medtronic can continue to evolve, always on assignment to contribute to human welfare.

Alone, each one of us can make a difference;
together we are unstoppable.
—Pramila Jayapal, director of The Hate Free
Zone Campaign of Washington

TOP-DOWN SOLUTIONS
FOR DEFINING PURPOSE

Rain forest or mangrove swamp . . . as individuals and as corporations, we can begin to understand our purposes and develop our corporate calling by crafting answers to three key questions in the same manner as the Faithful Managers—those employees who understood their assignments and carried out the wishes of their CEO.

WHOSE COMPANY IS IT?

Does your company belong to the management team? To the stockholders? To the employees? To the community? If you want to be on assignment, it needs to belong to God.

How does that work? A friend of ours is president of a retail firm. One morning as he took time to pray, a thought filled his mind again and again: "Whose company is it?" He said, "Lord, I appreciate so much the way you are helping me in my personal life as I try to build a solid family, but I can handle the business on my own. However, if I need help, I'll come to you."

Again, a voice seemed to ask, "Whose business is it?" Our friend got the message and turned over his business dealings to God. This change in outlook means that he asks for God's influence before making decisions, keeping his corporate calling front and center each day at the office.

WHO IS CRAFTING THE VISION?

Good stewards try to base their decisions on what they believe their employers would decide. Hopefully they've had frequent dialogues about that vision and the steward understands it.

If you accept that your company can be a conduit for bigger purposes, then your vision for it will also stem from a dialogue with its true owner, the Lord. Instead of passive consent ("Hey, God, this is what we want to be, but let us know if you have something different in mind . . ."), strive to receive your vision ("Lord, help us see the possibilities you have in mind . . .").

The difference can be as striking as the Israelites' first visions of the promised land.[23] A dozen spies were sent to explore Canaan and report back on the quality of the land as well as the strength of their enemies. Ten of the men saw only the strong fortifications and reported back, "We can't win against the inhabitants; they are too strong."

Joshua and Caleb, the other two spies, looked at the land through God's promise that it would belong to Israel. Their report? "If the Lord is pleased with us, he will lead us into that land, a land flowing with milk and honey, and will give it to us."[24] They stuck with the vision they'd been given.

The Joshuas and Calebs of the business world disregard the glum reports of their colleagues who believe that the only way to be successful in business is to be reminded daily of the dog-eat-dog nature of the marketplace. They stake out their corporate callings and watch them become reality.

HOW WILL YOUR MEASUREMENTS ALIGN WITH YOUR VISION?

Perhaps you think your company's vision is already in alignment with the concepts of stewardship. It may be, but constant rethinking of the assumptions you used while developing it can point out inconsistencies and, in some cases, false assumptions. Often the inconsistencies revolve around incentives. Are you measuring success by the acquiring myth or by your corporate calling?

For corporations, the mindset switch needs to be around how success is viewed. Success may not be building the biggest or fastest-growing or most innovative corporation—that's the path of the mangrove swamp. Instead, success can be measured by finding the most appropriate, exciting, fulfilling niche and excelling at what that niche requires—the path of the rain forest.

Jim Collins, author of *Good to Great: Why Some Companies Make the Leap . . . and Others Don't*[25] calls it the "Hedgehog Concept," reflecting that hedgehogs only have one trick in their survival toolkit: rolling into a ball to deflect predators with their quills. It works so well that hedgehogs don't need other defense strategies. Collins found that great companies have found their own hedgehog trick—that core proficiency on which they can build their success. Hedgehog companies, instead of growing randomly, relate everything back to that core proficiency, building their core business at the intersection of the following goals:

- What they are deeply passionate about
- What drives their economic engine (i.e., a profit can be made)
- What they can be best in the world at

Collins points out that the hedgehog concept does not mean aiming to be the best, but having "an understanding of what you can be the best at. The distinction is absolutely crucial."[26]

Think again back to the Faithful Managers. They weren't measured against everyone else's success, but against the progress they'd made with what they'd been given. While businesses must be aware of their competitors and changes in the marketplace, focusing on a hedgehog concept—such as "making the world a better place by inspiring people to celebrate life" or "saving lives"—will let your corporate calling be the driving force of your business.

ENVISIONING YOUR CORPORATE BEST
First a few "don'ts" for discovering your company's corporate calling.

Don't retreat; advance. Author Len Sweet hosts "advances," not "retreats," where you prepare yourself to go forward in life.[27] Instead of the traditional withdrawal from the realities of corporate life (e.g., a three-day executive retreat), immerse yourself in the reality of your customers and competitors and suppliers. What needs to be done? What is missing? What could you do better? As Paul Hawken puts it, "Your business must be an extension of who you are and what you are trying to learn and achieve. You know that you want to replace, improve, or change. Begin where the tool breaks, the service slips, or the shoe pinches."[28]

Don't start with products or services. Go to a higher level of purpose: What do you want to do for the world? Perhaps your assignment will fill a small niche, such as comfortable footwear that will make people happier. Perhaps your assignment will extend beyond your current imagination, such as WorldWise wanting to help change the world. The point is to be wary of defining a mission that will become obsolete in a world that is changing at the speed of microchips (soon to be nano-chips).

Don't start at the top. Involve people from as many layers of your company as you can. When Jane facilitated strategic planning for small-town banks, she gathered the whole staff. Often, the tellers knew more than the loan officers about what people in town wanted, needed, or were thankful for. An "If only we could . . ." statement might just change how you view your assignment.

This doesn't mean that the vision comes from the bottom, but rather the vision is influenced by the bottom. Input comes from listening to all stakeholders, all the while listening to receive the assignment from our Creator.

Don't worry about how you'll accomplish the vision. The important thing is to understand what you can and can't change. For example, 150 years ago, European doctors considered as normal the 20 percent mortality rate due to childbed fever for mothers who gave birth in hospitals. They couldn't expect better outcomes.

One man, Ignaz Semmelweiss, disagreed. Once he resolved that having one in five mothers die was unacceptable, he set about to change reality. His vision of more mothers surviving to care for their children led him to look for causes of infection. He didn't have to look far. Medical students on the ward with the highest mortality rate had a regular routine: examine childbirth fever victims in the morgue, then deliver babies, without washing their hands. (While scientists had studied germs through a microscope, no one believed that anything so small could affect anything as big as a human being.)

No one saw the connection until Semmelweis questioned the prevailing mindset. When Semmelweis required that the students on his ward wash their hands in a solution of carbonated lime before examining patients, the mortality rate dropped to less than 2 percent. That's the power of understanding what you want to achieve.

DESIGNER COMPANIES

Instead of embarking on a "visioning" process or "strategic planning," pretend you are a corporate "designer." Before interior designers make a single recommendation to a client, they listen for how the room or building is to be used. A conversation over a living room might go like this:

"Will you be entertaining? How often? What will be the size of the groups?"

"Will this be a formal space or do you need room for children to wrestle?"

"How important is TV? How big of a screen will you want?"

"Will you serve food or drinks here? Do you need buffet space or will that happen in a different part of the house?"

Answers to these questions define everything from the quality of carpet to the style of furniture the designer might suggest. The same is true of a company; the design starts with what you plan to use it for. It's the foundation for all you will do.

While there is no perfect way to envision your company's assignment, there are some key questions to ask. The bigger the questions, the better. It's time to think of the unanswerable, then allow time to see what answers you generate.

What is our ongoing mission? Like the companies in the oil company study, what core mission extends beyond the life of your products or the upheaval of your marketplace?

For example, General Electric's mission is to improve the quality of life through technology and innovation. There's always a next step in that mission. Likewise for the Joseph Company's mission of helping the oppressed, and for WorldWise's desire to change the world.

How would things change if we succeeded? What would be different about your products or services, the environment, your community, or whatever part of your circle of influence you wish to have the greatest impact on?

Be as specific as you can. In working with a team of teachers at an urban school, Jane encouraged them to envision how their students would change if the program changes they were implementing were truly successful. Their vision? That their students would become "excited, motivated learners who understand how they learn best and who choose to do more than the minimum because they are engaged." The vision then became the measure of success. Lesson plans succeeded if the students dived into the materials or if they asked (as several did), "Can we complete two of the projects instead of just one?"

How does this mission stand up? Imagine some different scenarios. Is your assignment broad enough to cover changes?

Could changes in laws, for any reason, fundamentally change the way you do business, as happened to real estate investment trusts in the late 1980s?

Could demand for your products or services change exponentially, as happened in the computer industry? A key executive in a now defunct company said in the 1970s, "Why would anyone want a computer in their home?"

Could globalization turn your market upside down?

The goal isn't to fit the vision to the most probable future, but to see how well it holds up under a variety of predictions and then make adjustments.

Does this mission provide meaning for employees? Work takes up most of our lives. If we cannot find meaning and purpose at work, our struggle to find it elsewhere can die before it begins.

The exponential increase in executive salaries may be an indicator of how little meaning they find in their work. Derek Bok, the former president of Harvard University, suggests that the drive for short-term profits required of top corporate executives requires that they overlook everything else—even the needs of employees and the community. "In short, top executives have to be paid outrageous salaries to motivate them not to yield to their instincts toward social responsibility.[29] It takes vast sums of money before it becomes a substitute for meaning.

One company that helped employees find meaning is Interface Corporation, a carpet manufacturer. The chairman, Ray Anderson, read *The Ecology of Commerce* by Paul Hawken and decided that they had to change the way they do business to stop the cycle of waste. Now instead of selling carpet, they lease it, taking it back when it is worn out, and recycling it. He says, "I have asked my people to join with me in leading the second industrial revolution because the first is not sustainable."[30] That's a purpose that can bring people to work.

It's also a rain forest purpose, not a mangrove swamp. One way to translate the ancient Chinese characters for "business" are as "life" and "meaning." A rain forest company can give its employees, investors, customers, and communities both life and meaning. A mangrove company simply chases the acquiring myth.

Rain forest corporations fit within the vision of corporate calling, acting on a vision bigger than growth. As we've seen, entertainment companies, manufacturing firms, wholesalers, service industries—corporations of varying shapes and sizes—can envision themselves as rain forest companies.

John Sherrill tells the story of Mr. Rossi, a wall builder. Born in Sicily, Mr. Rossi was apprenticed at the age of seven and, after moving to the United States, continued to craft stone walls well into his seventies. His goal was nothing less than building perfect walls in an environment where all too many workers easily settled for second best. However, Mr. Rossi's reaction to the shoddy workmanship of others was sorrow rather than disgust. When faced with a wall that was crumbling because the original builder hadn't properly filled a crack with cement, Mr. Rossi said, "I don't curse him. I ask God to bless him. Think what that work do to him here." He put his hand over his heart. Then he took his hat off and added, "You will bless him, God?"

John concluded, "I am sure that I shall never again see poor workmanship without remembering that prayer. Nor shall I see good work without remembering Mr. Rossi."[31]

The right vision helps corporations create good works and rain forest richness, bringing fulfillment to the hearts and souls of employees as they work toward a God-given corporate calling.

BOTTOM-UP STRATEGIES FOR DEFINING PURPOSE

When I put the plate down, you don't hear a sound. When I pick up a glass, I want it to be just right. When someone says, "How come you're just a waitress?" I say, "Don't you think you deserve being served by me?"
—Delores Dante, waitress[32]

When people ask you, "What do you do?" how do you answer?

If your job disappeared tomorrow, would you be as comfortable with your answer? Understanding the nature of your corporate calling, not just your job, is a key element in being able to influence the vision of others.

People like Delores Dante, quoted above, know that they are far more than just their jobs. They have personal visions that stretch beyond what they are required to do, much as rain forest companies have visions bigger than profit-taking.

Delores didn't consider herself "just a waitress." When Studs Terkel interviewed her in the 1970s, she'd been working at the same restaurant for over twenty years. She admitted that she took the job out of desperation—her husband left her with three children and debts—but to her, the job was more than serving food. She said, "Everyone wants to eat, everyone has hunger. And I serve them. If they've had a bad day, I nurse them, cajole them. Maybe with coffee I give them a little philosophy. They have cocktails, I give them political science."

Delores knew that she was much more than a waitress. And her philosophy of separating what she did from her job description turned waitressing into a corporate calling.

YOUR PERSONAL VISION

That's the key. You have a corporate calling that somehow links what you do best with the needs of the world. Setting aside the acquiring myth, you find your own mission that helps you to live out the words of the apostle Paul: "Do not be conformed to this world, but be transformed by the renewing of your minds, so that you may discern what is the will of God—what is good and acceptable and perfect."[33]

Your purpose may or may not propel you toward social causes or radical actions. It may involve simply saying, "How can I carry out my calling where I'm currently employed?"

But before you can ask that, you need to identify your calling. At the start of our *LifeKeys* classes we tell people, "Please don't expect that you'll leave here with a life plan. You might, but it might take six to nine months to understand what you do best and why you're here. It took the two of us at least that long."

For Jane, knowing her assignment brings harmony to her different "jobs" as a writer, a corporate trainer, and a consultant to schools on learning styles strategies. In each case, Jane is "helping others reach their full potential, giving them tools and models to successfully continue the process on their own"—a mission statement that she pondered for three years before being able to write it down.

For David, whether as a pastor or as a consultant, he is "envisioning, communicating, and living out a model of what it means to be a Christian man, to have an impact on and empower as many people as I can, as deeply as I can, for as long as I can, to further the kingdom of God." He spent almost nine months crafting his statement, which also includes the values he hopes to model. Having it down on paper helps David choose wisely among the many things he would love to do.

If you find yourself saying, "No, I'm really just a waitress," then sit down with someone who listens to you. Jane will never forget counseling one *LifeKeys* facilitation workshop attendee who told her the following:

- The other two people from her church would be the "real" teachers of *LifeKeys* the next fall. She wasn't on staff.
- She was only there because the other two struggled to get along with each other.
- She didn't have any talents. She was just an office worker.

Jane kept asking questions until she discovered that the woman's friends, neighbors, and coworkers frequently asked her to do the following:

- Listen when they had conflicts, helping them see past differences in opinion.
- Fix anything from a toaster to a tractor. Besides repair work, she had built custom furniture.
- Help them organize closets, drawers, and filing systems. She was so good at this that friends often sent her to home organization stores with a blank check saying, "Get whatever you think I need."

After Jane assured this woman that not everyone could listen, fix, or organize, together they crafted the following calling: "I want to be the hands and ears of God to those around me. The woman burst into tears as she realized that she could do God's work as an office worker, a neighbor, and a friend."

Finding a vision for your own assignment is similar to how a corporation can identify its "Hedgehog Concept":

- Ponder what you are deeply passionate about. Try thinking globally *and* locally.
- Consider how it fits into your world of work, assuming you need a source of income. Can you carry out your corporate calling in the midst of your job or will your job support you so that you can carry it out elsewhere?
- Limit your ideas to things that you can do better than anyone else. This isn't bragging, but like the woman who "just fixed things," admitting that you have an assignment to do your best with what you have.

Another way to think of it is to imagine life *without* your current job or career. What would you still want to do? At its core, what gives you meaning? The answer may not be obvious.

For example, at first glance, being an electrician is about making things, working with your hands, and solving problems. Renay Poirer of Eau Claire, Wisconsin, found out that it's about much more. Back in 1990, he lost his sight in an industrial accident. He could no longer work as an electrician and had to find a new way to help support his family. He missed his coworkers, his customers, being busy, and always feeling needed. Then it dawned on him. What he missed most was being able to help other people. He could do that in many jobs besides being an electrician. After careful evaluation, Renay took on the challenge of attending college for the first time and becoming a physical therapy assistant. Renay's *job* changed from electrician to physical therapy assistant, but his *purpose* stayed the same: helping others. When his sight returned after ten years of darkness (the doctors were not sure whether regaining his sight was just mysterious or fully miraculous), he stuck to physical therapy work, which had become as fulfilling as his former career.[34]

Another path to personal vision is considering whether there is something no one else can do or wants to do. Maybe you're the one who creates community by planning company picnics. Or you ask the questions no one else dares voice. Or perhaps your job is merely a conduit for something far more significant than you ever imagined. Oskar Schindler of *Schindler's List* fame, for example, thought of himself as a businessman. Before the war, few would have found much to admire in him:

> He married Emilie Schindler at nineteen, but was never without a mistress or two. Hard drinking and feckless, he had the soul of a gambler, winning big and losing bigger. He had presided over the demise of his family business and become a salesman when opportunity came knocking in the guise of the war.
>
> Never one to miss a chance to make money, he marched into Poland on the heels of the SS. He dived headfirst into the black-market and the underworld and soon made friends with the local Gestapo bigwigs, softening them up with women, money and illicit booze. His newfound connections helped him acquire a factory which he ran with the cheapest labor around: Jewish.[35]

Yet when Schindler realized that the Germans would not ship to the death camps any Jewish workers on his payroll, his enamelware factory changed from a business to a place of refuge. He worked to save his Jewish workers and as his wife described him, "He seemed absolutely uninterested in anything having to do with the factory, except that thanks to its existence a few lives could be saved."[36] He traded away the wealth he'd accumulated, bribing the SS with diamonds, caviar, cigarettes, cognac, and other black-market items to protect his people. He never ran another successful business, but because of his "hedgehog" concentration, over thirteen hundred Jews survived Hitler's terror.

Are there opportunities you're missing because you can't see how they fit with your corporate calling? Or, like Renay, could you move from electricity to physical therapy? Are you missing assignments because they don't seem to be part of your job or, like Oskar Schindler, could you move from business owner to lifesaver?

New possibilities open up when you move toward being more than just your job and toward your calling. How would headlines have read if more people at the companies in the most recent round of scandals had hedgehog concepts around ethical standards?

SPREADING THE VISION

Few of us have the power to set the vision of an organization. In large corporations, the vision comes from a handful at the top, perhaps with the help of representatives from different departments and levels of responsibility. In small businesses, the owner may only ask for input from a few advisors.

But even if you are far from the inner power circles, you still have circles of influence. If you feel helpless to change your company's vision, think of what you *can* change. If you work for a company whose vision brings to mind the mangrove swamp, remember that instead of asking, "How can *I* do anything?" a better response is, "Yes, I have to do something."

If everyone around you thinks they're "only waitresses," what would happen if you got them to believe, "If I treat my customers like they're the most important people in the world, they just might have kinder words for others."

Or if every division in your company is in competition with every other division, what if you worked to get those closest to you to begin cooperating?

Or if your company focuses on money and nothing else, what if you got two, then three, then more of your coworkers to join together for community service? Would people start to yearn for a purpose beyond a paycheck?

Your hedgehog concept just might be laying aside your dismay over the corporate mangrove swamp vision and turning your circle of influence into its own rain forest environment. What would it look like? Employees would work together, each assigned to the tasks he or she does best. Cooperation, not competition, would permeate the atmosphere. Even with minimal resources, everyone would find ways to give to each other. And the work could flourish. Maybe the finance department becomes an "honesty" hedgehog. Maybe the customer service department becomes a "golden rule" hedgehog. Maybe the maintenance department becomes a "best practices" department. Maybe the claims department becomes the "customer is always right" department.

The key? If your company's vision is no more than "Get as big as we can to make as much as we can," no matter how nicely it's worded, your department can still take a different path. Can we find a mission that's bigger than our function? Can we influence others if we succeed? Can this vision bring meaning to our team? Can we make a difference, even if it's only incremental? You might not change the world, or even your company, but your circle of influence might be bigger than you think.

Take a banker, for example. Banks, through the Community Reinvestment Act, are supposed to work to meet the credit needs of the businesses and neighborhoods around them, but they are primarily financial institutions, with visions of financial products and services.

One bank president, however, saw another vision. He recruited a man who worked around the corner from the bank, at the neighborhood YMCA, and told him, "Why don't you come on board with us and do the same thing you've been doing at the Y? Of course you'll have to go to lending school, but . . ."

The man agreed because he envisioned how the bank would be a better platform than the Y for his real vision—trying to get businesses, citizens, and public officials in the community to come together to deal with important issues. Over the next years, they tackled issues such as unemployment; renewing the look, feel, and spirit of the neighborhood; turning old industrial sites into new enterprises; and having fun as a community.

Did it work? Picture a bank as the command post for over a thousand volunteers—Boy Scouts, church groups, school clubs, service organizations, corporate employee teams—all working to renovate a hundred homes of elderly people in the neighborhood in a single day. Picture coordinating the supplies for painting, roofing, carpentry, cement patching, yard work, electrical repairs, window replacement, and rubbish disposal. Picture assigning the different teams to sites that matched their skills. Picture coordinating food and transportation and communication and fellowship.

Then picture a dance at the local high school that Saturday night, attended by all the volunteers to celebrate finishing every single house targeted by Project NEAT: North East [neighborhood] All Together. And they *were* all together, the entire neighborhood participating in a modern-day barn-raising extravaganza.

A bank can be much more than a mangrove swamp if just a few people have a different vision, such as "Our bank can be the heart of the community, getting people to work together." Now that's a rain forest vision that can flourish.

If the world were going along smoothly, if life were growing easier,
it wouldn't matter so much which way we were turning.
But most of us feel that the world is deteriorating. . . .
We can turn away, or we can turn toward.
Those are the only two choices we have.
—Margaret Wheatley[37]

CHAPTER 4

PROFITS

THE SACRED COW OF BUSINESS

To be clever enough to get all that money,
one must be stupid enough to want it.
      —G. K. Chesterton[1]

T HE NIGHT OF DECEMBER 11, 1995, AARON FEUERSTEIN WAS
STILL chuckling over his surprise seventieth birthday party
when, while turning a corner, he nearly slammed into a late-night
traffic jam. As he hit his brakes, he saw flames shooting from the
windows of the old mill complex, while thick black smoke jarred by
giant fireballs billowed toward the stars.

It was Malden Mills going up in smoke, his textile mill, inherited from his father, founded by his grandfather. The largest
employer in Lawrence, Massachusetts, with over three thousand
workers. The inferno completely destroyed three key production
buildings.

The next day, Feuerstein met with fire officials, surveyed the
ruins, and listened in wonder to tales of thirty-six of his workers
who had battled the blaze all night long to save the just-completed

Polartec finishing plant. With that facility, and new state-of-the-art machinery that hadn't yet been unloaded from delivery trucks, production could continue.

But rumors were already spreading through Lawrence: Feuerstein was too old to rebuild. He'd take the insurance money and retire—or rebuild down South where labor was cheap. The town wouldn't survive.

Feuerstein put out the word that he would speak to employees that night at Lawrence's Central Catholic High School. There, he told a stunned crowd, "We will rebuild. And your paychecks will continue for at least the next month. There will be no layoffs."

To Feuerstein, his employees were his most important asset, not the buildings. In a speech at MIT, he said, "You can have the best engineers, the best research and development guy, the best technical expert figure out how to get better quality. But in the last analysis, it is the man on the floor who is going to get that quality for you. If he feels he is a part of the enterprise and he feels he is treated the way he should be treated, he will go the extra mile to provide that quality."[2]

Eventually, full pay was extended to Malden Mills' employees for ninety days. Eighty-five percent of the employees were back at work within four months. Putting their ingenuity to work for the company that had kept them on the payroll, they managed to increase production output by almost 77 percent in the remaining plant building.

Since then, Feuerstein has been showcased in the media and showered with awards as a model of a CEO who acts on his values. To all of the attention, he says, "Fifty years ago, nothing would have been thought about somebody who rebuilt his factory after it was burned, who worried about his people and his community. Today a nerve has been struck, shocking people into the realization that the country is going in the wrong direction . . ."[3]

He's right. He's received thousands of letters from people who wish they could work for a company that values its values more than its profits.

Lesser known, however, is the rest of the story. Insurance covered only 75 percent of the costs of rebuilding Malden Mills, partly because of the continuation of worker wages and because Feuerstein insisted on designing the new buildings with the latest in energy-efficient technology, excellent air quality control, natural daylight to create a positive atmosphere, and cutting-edge equipment. With market pressures from foreign competitors and Polartec imitations, Malden Mills was forced into Chapter 11 bankruptcy proceedings in November 2001. The lead counsel for the firm's creditors at the time said that Feuerstein should be replaced. In a *Harvard Business Review* article called "The Virtue Matrix," the author said, "Feuerstein spared [employees] considerable hardship—but his generous act decreased his own wealth and that of his fellow shareholders. . . . Feuerstein's conduct probably won't become the norm in corporate America."[4]

But isn't Feuerstein's ethic the norm that we want? Where corporations consider the interests of not just their shareholders, but the other stakeholders: employees, the community, their customers, our environment? Proponents of this view call it corporate social responsibility. Opponents say it simply isn't the business of business.

WHAT IS THE BUSINESS OF BUSINESS?

In 1970 Milton Friedman, an Economics Nobel laureate, published an article in *New York Times Magazine* titled, "The Social Responsibility of Business Is to Increase Its Profits." He concluded the article with a quote from his book *Capitalism and Freedom*: "There is one and only one social responsibility of business—to use its resources and engage in activities designed to increase its profits so long as it stays within the rules of the game, which is to say, engages in open and free competition without deception or fraud."[5]

Proponents of Friedman's views center their rhetoric around the belief, "What's good for business is good for the country." They believe that creating conditions that allow businesses to thrive means more jobs, more income taxes in the government coffers, more capital investment, higher stock prices, and therefore higher 401(k) values for the rest of us. Based on these beliefs, local governments provide tax incentives, subsidize sports stadiums, and provide attractive funding options to lure new businesses to locate within their city limits. Taxpayers are told that increased jobs and revenue streams will eventually make up for higher taxes.

The legal system of the United States is definitely on Friedman's side—every state has a statute worded approximately like this: "The directors and officers of a corporation shall exercise their powers and discharge their duties with a view to the interests of the corporation and of the shareholders." If the directors and officers don't, shareholders can and do file suit.

Legally, there is no responsibility to the public interest. Further, executives are pressured to do only one thing: make money. This mandate may explain the often-seen disparity between what business executives espouse as personal values and how they make business decisions.[6]

However, another position on profits is possible, that profits can't be made at the expense of other stakeholders: employees, the community, the environment, or customers. This position seems so inherently right to thousands, if not millions of Americans, that a grassroots effort to help Malden Mills began when news of its financial difficulties surfaced, difficulties that had come from the socially responsible decision of Feuerstein to value employees above stockholders. People started a campaign to encourage the purchase of genuine Polartec products during the 2002 Christmas season. Others mailed checks of up to one thousand dollars to reduce the debt load (all of the donations were in turn donated by Malden Mills in the form of blankets for children in need).

In effect, these people are saying, "We want businesses to be socially responsible, sharing their wealth with employees as well as using their power to work against poverty, pollution, ignorance, ugliness in our society." Picketing efforts, media campaigns, boycotts, and shareholder groups pressing for change are all signs of the push for corporate social responsibility.

Friedman disagreed with the premises of social responsibility. He believed that any attempt by corporate executives to use business proceeds for agendas, such as reducing pollution more than required or hiring hard-core unemployed workers, was the same as imposing taxes on stockholders—and only the government had the right to impose such taxes.

Further, he thought that "social engineering" should take place through democratic processes, not through the decisions of corporate executives whose responsibility is to the people who hired them, not to the welfare of society. After all, if stockholders share the sentiments of the executives, they can donate their dividends and capital gains to social causes—or become activists for change.

Sometimes the markets work as Friedman proposed: One of the major factors behind the halting of construction of nuclear power plants was the market reality that citizens refused to purchase the bonds issued to finance them. Worried about the risks, investors voted "no" with their wallets to nuclear power. That spoke louder than the protests.

To some, however, waiting for markets to reflect such movements takes too long. Further, they are all too aware that corporations have sizeable clout. They can do great good more quickly than individuals, and they can do great damage.

The cry for corporate social responsibility also includes the opinion that "Businesses are greedy, corrupt, and need to be regulated and controlled." Certainly, Enron, Arthur Andersen, and others have supplied this side with considerable supporting evidence in recent years. As we've seen, when the acquiring myth becomes the driving force of a corporation, even the ethics that Friedman insisted on, staying "within the rules of the game, which is to say, engages in open and free competition without deception or fraud," seem to fall by the wayside.

How do we balance the need for profits and the need to remember that other stakeholders count? Can corporations be socially responsible in ways other than earning as much as they can?

A DIFFERENT KIND OF ROI

It's true that by definition, we invest to make a monetary return, but hopefully a lesson was learned during the last stock market cycle: If returns are unbelievably high, they probably are not to be believed. Further, not just the corporate executives in the few highly publicized scandals were guilty, but everyone who participated in the market boom looking for high returns was guilty of the massive greed that pushed the market ever higher—until it crashed. To point out the obvious, Enron stated in its 2000 annual report that it was laser-focused on earnings per share. And that laser blinded everyone to the shadow games that produced those earnings.

One might say that Feuerstein at Malden Mills was more interested in a new kind of ROI, a return on *integrity* rather than on *investment*. People who knew Feuerstein well said that his actions after the fire weren't an anomaly but illustrative of how he lived. His values are his foundation. Feuerstein is an Orthodox Jew who believes that his business needs to follow the precepts of Moses: "Do not take advantage of a hired man who is poor and needy, whether he is a brother Israelite or an alien living in one of your towns."[7]

His business philosophy also illustrates how Jesus meant for us to live: "[E]veryone who hears these words of mine and puts them into practice is like a wise man who built his house on the rock. The rain came down, the streams rose, and the winds blew and beat against that house; yet it did not fall, because it had its foundation on the rock."

Note that Jesus's parable doesn't say "if" the rains come. It says they will come, as sure as the fires came to Malden Mills. Building on rock means we can still survive the storm, unlike the person who builds on sand: "[E]veryone who hears these words of mine and does not put them into practice is like a foolish man who built his house on sand. The rain came down, the streams rose, and the winds blew and beat against that house, and it fell with a great crash."[8]

Businesses built on sand might seem healthy, successful, marvels of innovation. However, the nature of their foundations is revealed when the storms come, storms like the end of a market boom.

The bull market of the 1990s was billed as one of the greatest periods of wealth creation ever, with estimates as high as $10 to $15 trillion in new money before the market downturn. By March 2000, 60 percent of all Americans had money in the stock market. That percentage hadn't been so high since 1929, when Joe Kennedy Sr. reportedly pulled his money out of the market after receiving a market tip from his shoeshine boy (and *Forbes* magazine was quoting this story as a warning as early as August 1999).

Some people saw the sand from the start. Billionaire Wall Street investor Warren Buffett refused to invest in tech stocks because he couldn't see how they were making true profits. Likening their business model to old-fashioned chain letters, he said, "The fact is that a bubble market has allowed the creation of bubble companies, entities designed more with an eye to making money *off* investors rather than *for* them."[9]

Not all of the "winners" set out to create losers. Many simply had incredibly good ideas that grew with unprecedented speed as technology boomed and the Internet took off. When these first companies created tremendous wealth for their founders, some people even argued that perhaps the rapid pace of change made designing "built to last" companies an outdated concept. They suggested "built to flip" as the modern alternative—companies designed for rapid growth so they could quickly be sold to the highest bidder.

The "built to flip" label comes from the dot-com IPO ("initial public offering") roller-coaster ride. With technology advancing at lightning speed, many entrepreneurs founded small, shoestring companies to develop one or two computer or Internet-related products or services. "Flippable" companies were the small start-ups that could be, and in some cases were designed to be, quickly sold to larger players. Perhaps being "built to flip" or to grow quickly, then sell out, was a good strategy for economic efficiency; however, hindsight shows that "built on sand" is a better description of many of those companies.

Early start-ups, such as Hotmail and Netscape, created new niche products that the big players including Cisco and Microsoft wanted. From the viewpoint of the buyers, acquiring flippable companies often made more economic sense than developing the products through their own research and development departments.

But after several highly publicized, lucrative "flips," as when Microsoft acquired Hotmail for $400 million in Microsoft shares, it seemed as if everyone wanted to get in on the dot-com boom. What happened next was not so much the actions of criminals but of opportunists. Analysts, experts, and attorneys for the losers in this fiasco are now arguing about how much wealth was actually created and what was merely transferred to a relatively small number of individuals who took advantage of a hot market. Jim Collins, author of *Built to Last,* calls it a "built-to-flip mindset: opportunists who created a significant delta between short-term share price and long-term share value and then cashed out before the gap could close."[10]

While there were some cases of fraud, the broader pattern was an incredible influx of capital into the tech stocks market, enough so that funds were available for literally any start-up with the magic words of "dot-com" or "tech" in their proposals.

Richard Moore, treasurer for the state of North Carolina, was one of the few funds managers who stuck to proven strategies for investment throughout the 1990s; his funds were scarcely affected by the market crash. He described the boom this way:

> [Eighty million Americans] have been enticed—and I will use that word again—they have been enticed through tax policy and professional advice to participate and share in the American dream. Now, it is not [Congress's] job, nor is it the job of corporate America, to ensure that that dream comes true. However, it is [Congress's] job to make sure that the marketplace is fair to all so some don't profit and others lose—from the exact same investment.[11]

How were so many Americans enticed into the market? Encouraged by financial advisors and headlines filled with stories of the newly rich, these new investors forgot—or never learned—or were blinded by greed to—the fundamental principles of investing: due diligence and diversity. In other words, buyer beware and look before you leap.

However, most of the actions by the initial investors carried out Friedman's maxim of "there is one and only one social responsibility of business—to use its resources and engage in activities designed to increase its profits so long as it stays within the rules of the game, which is to say, engages in open and free competition without deception or fraud."[12]

Friedman's ideas surrounding increasing profits assume, though, that the market players are operating in a moral manner, operating without deception or fraud. The ethical dot-com designers can be differentiated from the "flippers" by looking at what happened to those who didn't understand "the rules of the game." There was nothing socially responsible about the profits generated while others lost out on the same investments.

This unprecedented foray into free markets for so many people didn't spread the wealth the way it was promised by "market fundamentalists" (people who believe that markets run with minimal governmental interference create the greatest economic prosperity for all). Why not?

Because without moral principles, markets don't work as the market fundamentalists envision. As we look ahead to the next market cycle, finding a way to build on rock seems like a good idea. Further, building on rock is exactly what Adam Smith, who is frequently misinterpreted by market fundamentalists, had in mind.

ANOTHER VIEW OF THINGS

Tug-o-wars over economic principles often begin with the eighteenth-century economist Adam Smith. He is often cited for championing laissez-faire markets, the model espoused by market fundamentalists. He didn't. To better understand Smith, one needs to know that he saw economics as a means to improve human character. His two main works, *An Inquiry into the Nature and Causes of the Wealth of Nations* and *The Theory of Moral Sentiments,* together put forth his ideas.

Instead of advocating laissez-faire markets, Smith showed why a market economy, where people can bring their goods or find employers for their labor, might best meet the needs of consumers—provided that weaker players were protected. Some of his main points include the following:

1. The division of labor lets workers be more productive. Smith wasn't referring to the factory assembly-line extreme, but to the simple principle that being self-sufficient can be very inefficient. For example, because Jane can buy her groceries at the store rather than having to plant crops and milk cows, she has more time to write.
2. Smith advocated natural liberty, but this doesn't translate to total lack of government restraint on the market. Smith referred to natural liberty as the freedom to control one's own passions. In the language of his times, "natural" referred both to fact and to the way things ought to be. Because humans struggle to control greed, pride, and power, Smith advocated that this "freedom" be learned from such social institutions as the market, the family, religious communities, and the law.[13]

3. Smith stated clearly that governments needed to have a *visible* hand in the markets, ensuring justice and fairness, creating social structures, such as education and law enforcement, providing for defense and protection of private property, and building the transportation systems and utilities necessary for commerce. Sufficient taxes would be necessary to pay for these necessities.

4. To measure the success of the market, Smith wanted legislators to concentrate on the purchasing power of wages as the true test of how people are faring. Not ROI, not GDP (gross domestic product), not consumer confidence, not inventory levels.

5. Smith's *invisible* hand of the market so often referenced nowadays referred to the fact that when all of these other elements were met, the markets were efficient at allocating capital and wealth.

To put it mildly, our markets don't look much like Adam Smith's vision of free markets. To put it truthfully,

> the "invisible hand" is regularly moved, shaken, deflected, squeezed, tilted, twisted and bent by governments which in turn are subjected to a variety of pressures and forces which distort the outcomes. Whether it is corporations or unions, self-interest is frequently expressed in ways which alter the achievement of the "greatest good for the greatest number." In such cases, the critical difficulty is who defines the common good and who determines the locus of responsibility for creating the undesirable situation and for correcting it.[14]

ANCIENT BUSINESS ETHICS

Again, we are not arguing that profits are immoral. Remember the parable of the Faithful Managers? The manager who had five talents and produced a 100 percent ROI was told, "Well done, good and faithful servant! You have been faithful with a few things; I will put you in charge of many things. Come and share your master's happiness!"[15]

However, an overview of different biblical texts suggests that there is some upward limit on profits. When Joshua led his people into the promised land, God instructed them to divide up the land among the twelve tribes, giving each family enough to make a living. Everyone started out equally, but God knew that natural disasters, crop failures, illnesses, and other factors would cause some to have to sell their holdings or borrow from their neighbors to keep things going.

So God built into the "business plan" the Year of Jubilee—every fifty years, everyone was to return to their own property. Things became equal again. As radical as this sounds, archaeological evidence of royal edicts, dating from 2400 to 1600 BCE, shows that lands were redistributed and debts forgiven. Michael Hudson, a professor at the University of Missouri, points out that what we take for granted "was radically disturbing in archaic times . . . the idea of unrestrained wealth-seeking. It took thousands of years for the idea of progress to become inverted, to connote irreversible freedom for the wealthy to deprive the peasantry of their lands and personal liberty."[16]

While the Jubilee year idea was based in an agrarian society, we still keep elements in our laws that allow people and businesses a clean slate after bankruptcy.

Another set of laws centered around forgiving interest and principal on loans. God recognized that debt is a huge obstacle to overcome and gave instructions for debt to be forgiven. For example, " . . . if he does not acquire the means to repay him, what he sold will remain in the possession of the buyer until the Year of Jubilee. It will be returned in the Jubilee, and he can then go back to his property."[17] Again, everyone had enough.

Even with restoration of capital and forgiveness of debt, God recognized that some people would still be caught in poverty and made provisions: "When you reap the harvest of your land, do not reap to the very edges of your field or gather the gleanings of your harvest . . . leave them for the poor and the alien."[18]

The following texts help us see what God had in mind for capital and profit-taking:

• A return on investment is not only moral, but expected.
• God's aim is for everyone to have enough to sustain themselves. This isn't communism, where everything is equal, but a system where no one has too little.

- In determining the profit you can take, the plight of the poor is to be figured in. Some of the harvest goes to them.
- Everything we have comes from God: "The land must not be sold permanently, because the land is mine and you are but aliens and my tenants. Throughout the country that you hold as a possession, you must provide for the redemption of the land."[19] That means that what we earn we should lay back at the feet of the master so we can be shown what to do with it in the next round.

From the beginning, then, God's view of our business efforts involved being Faithful Managers, using the land as the Lord would have it used, including to fulfill our social responsibilities. This sounds a bit more like Adam Smith's original idea of the visible hand of government, but Friedman himself points out the difference between free markets and giving businesses free rein:

> [The businessman] has been hired by his stockholders, as it were, to make as much money for them as he can within the rules of the game. And if the rules of the game are that you go to Washington to get a special privilege, I can't blame them for doing that. I'm going to blame the rest of us for being so stupid and foolish as to let them get away with it.[20]

Yet, if we're the ones who are stupid when we let businesses pursue practices that harm us, why can't we pressure from inside for change? Is there really no justification for social responsibility or can we rethink the role of business? Remember, Friedman said that "the business of business is business" as long as everyone was following the rules of the game. Instead, Friedman's words have been used as an excuse to create one of the most uneven playing fields of all times.

A CLEAR DEFINITION OF SOCIAL RESPONSIBILITY

Social responsibility matches up to our corporate calling, to run our businesses with attention to the following five corporate callings:

- purpose
- profits
- products and places
- people
- our planet

A corporation's targets for ROI cannot come at the expense of the other callings; however, there is a continuum for each of these stewardships. At one extreme are companies who do no more than satisfy the laws around these five corporate callings. We think these stewardships hold corporations to a higher law than simple compliance—and most business ethicists would agree. As you'll see throughout *Working with Purpose*, this stance isn't necessarily adequate given changing conditions, knowledge, and public opinion.

At the other extreme are corporations such as Patagonia and The Body Shop whose missions specifically call them to influence the world. While we will say more about their unique operations in other chapters, we do not believe that all corporations are called to the kind of advocacy efforts that these companies pursue (any more than all Christians are called to be preachers). These companies fulfill a purpose, but they may not be a workable model for all businesses.

In between compliance and major advocacy is a lot of room to be socially responsible without being extreme. Some companies might focus on one or two of the corporate callings while being adequate in the others. Or they may define their social responsibilities in a narrower way.

But the main point is that social responsibility isn't about putting together a values statement or avoiding creating toxic waste sites or providing employee benefits. Instead it's a way of doing business that demonstrates a corporate calling.

A LEGAL PROBLEM TO ADDRESS

We've passed laws about working conditions, pollution limits, and antitrust considerations, but we haven't attempted to get at the heart of the problem: Our laws dictate that corporations seek profits.

Remember Aaron Feuerstein, whose continuance as CEO was threatened because he put the needs of employees before those of shareholders, stating that employees are a corporate asset, not an expense? In this case, which stakeholders were the most important: the employees in a basically one-industry town or the investors? It's a moral dilemma.

The American Law Institute's *Principles on Corporate Governance* explicitly allows for managerial actions "made on the basis of ethical considerations even when doing so would not enhance corporate profit or shareholder gain" (Sec. 2.01, cmt. H, 1994), but as seen above, shareholders can push back on whether ethical considerations were sufficient to warrant a drop in profits.

We could change that. We could make directors legally responsible to make profits, but not by hurting employees or by increasing costs to the public or by stomping on human rights, the environment, or other areas that are matters of public interest. Just change the statutes to read, "The directors and officers of a corporation shall exercise their powers and discharge their duties with a view to the interests of the corporation and of the shareholders, but not at the expense of the environment, human rights, the public safety, the communities in which the corporation operates, or the dignity of its employees."[21]

Isn't that what we all want? Are we fools, as Friedman says, for allowing corporations to do otherwise? A *Business Week*/Harris poll asked Americans which version of corporate duties they preferred. Ninety-five percent rejected the idea the businesses had only the purpose of making profits and instead chose: "Corporations should have more than one purpose. They also owe something to their workers and the communities in which they operate, and they should sometimes sacrifice some profit for the sake of making things better for their workers and communities."[22]

A SACRED COW MELTDOWN

Even though this rethinking of corporate duties seems necessary, we are not arguing that the greatest economic minds of our age are wrong, but rather that our society is focusing on the wrong measures and not factoring in certain assumptions.

Here are some thoughts to ponder:

Do Shareholders Only Care about ROI?

This may have been true during the 1990s, but things are changing. For one thing, people saw how temporary ROI can be. For another, the enormity of corporate power is becoming apparent to more and more people. The following could all be examples of the kind of undemocratic taxes Friedman opposed, but perhaps they demonstrate that shareholders value more than just personal gain.

- *Increase in socially responsible investments (SRI).* While over $13 billion flowed out of the market in the first nine months of 2002, the much smaller group of SRI mutual funds gained $600 million. Visit www.business-ethics.com for a full list of the criteria required for a fund to be considered socially responsible. This increase in SRI reflects not just their performance—over the past three years, 40 percent of these funds earned four- or five-star ratings from Morningstar, compared with 33 percent of all funds—but a genuine desire by many people to associate with companies who are doing good works.

  Nearly three-quarters of Americans say they consider social responsibility issues when making investment decisions, and 12 percent say they would buy stock in socially responsible companies even if it meant a lower return.
- *The number of companies that are designed to be socially responsible in the first place.* When Ben & Jerry's made its initial stock offering, the whole idea was so radical that underwriters wanted them to reduce the stated contribution to charities of 7 percent of pretax earnings. Ben and Jerry refused, saying that the kind of stockholders they wanted would approve of their donations. They had no trouble selling the stock.
- *The resources which companies now dedicate to promoting their socially responsible efforts.* While some of this is pure propaganda (a company we will not name spent fifty times as much on publicizing their donations than they had

donated to the charities!), it is also a response to the demands of consumers and investors who apparently are interested in corporate ethics. They want to know about any sweatshop labor before sporting a pair of tennis shoes—or about a company's use of natural resources before cashing that dividend check.

Nike, for example, to address criticisms about working conditions in their overseas manufacturing facilities, now posts independent audit reports on their corporate Web sites. Not all of the information is favorable to Nike, but they have found that honesty rather than denial helps them deal with protestors—and develop better ways to deal with the problems.

If these trends truly indicate that shareholders care about the makeup of ROI and not just the bottom line, then perhaps using businesses for socially responsible purposes becomes less of a taxation without representation—that is, possibly reducing the return to shareholders because of charitable contributions or going beyond compliance on environmental issues—than it seemed to Friedman thirty years ago.

Further, as we recover from the most recent wave of economic difficulties, corporations have a unique opportunity to change their vision, to make shareholders aware that from now on, they will be about more than profits. They can change their measures and give shareholders the chance to find new investments, while prices are low, or join with firms committed to living out a corporate calling. In that way, shareholders will know about any "taxes" on their income, just like the original shareholders in Ben & Jerry's did.

What If Being Socially Responsible More Truly Reflects the Cost of Business?

Many of the companies that strive to be more socially responsible try to reflect the true cost of doing business. If the cost of an automobile or a refrigerator does not reflect its eventual disposal cost, isn't that also a taxation without representation—of every consumer and tax-payer in the country—not just the user or shareholders?

What about companies where wages and benefits are so skimpy that employees and their families qualify for Medicaid?

This trend is driven not only by the increase in low-income service industry jobs but by the shift to contract employment ("temp jobs") for professionals. In industries such as technology and publishing, companies have fired professionals, then hired them on a contract basis, which decreases benefit costs. If companies are able to shift healthcare costs that way, isn't that a tax on the rest of us?

What about the social costs of overworked employees? One estimate for the United States quoted an annual cost of $200 billion for work-related stress.[23] One of the reasons companies can so easily avoid these costs is the way we measure economic productivity. Our gross domestic product (GDP) shows the total market value of goods and services produced during the year (before subtracting for depreciation or consumption of capital during production). GDP is considered one of the most important indicators of our economy's health. However, look at the list of economic transactions included in GDP:

- Profits that firms make from cleaning up toxic waste sites
- Construction of new prisons
- Weight-loss products
- Healthcare costs for victims of drunk driving (and for anything else)
- Attorney's fees for divorces, frivolous lawsuits, and criminal defense

Should these really be included in a measure of prosperity? By this accounting, hurricanes are wonderful events since the destruction will lead to more construction and damage clean-up. Hurricanes are better for us, under this measure, than family afternoons at the playground that create no economic transactions and are therefore not measured in GDP.

A way to refocus our economy on true costs is to set aside GDP and instead track GPI—genuine progress indicator. This measure, advocated by a group of economists with an organization called Redefining Progress, does two things:

- It adds to GDP the "invisible" productivity of home, parenting, and volunteer work.
- It subtracts from GDP such costs as commuting time, auto

accidents, crime (do we want the construction of more jails in our GDP as a good thing?), environmental damage, and much more.

Some market analysts are starting to pay attention to GPI (which, incidentally, has been falling steadily since 1973). This is not an idea from the radical fringe, but is being advocated in the *Atlantic Monthly,* by Stanford professors, and even in the Commerce Department. The Commerce Department in 1994 wanted to adjust GDP for depletion of oil and other nonrenewable resources, but Congress shut down the analysis effort rather than risk the wrath of strong lobby industries such as coal and oil.

What does this say about the measures of prosperity our political leaders use as they guide economic policy? The authors of the book *Affluenza* put it this way: "National vitality, like personal health and community health, is not really about PowerPoint graphs and mindless business-as-usual, but about real things like the health of people, places, natural capital, and future generations. At all levels of our society, it's time to schedule a holistic annual check-up."[24]

Does It Actually Cost More to Be Socially Responsible?
A *Harvard Business Review* article titled "The Competitive Advantage of Corporate Philanthropy" pointed out that social objectives versus economic objectives is a false dichotomy. Sometimes acting on social interests improves economic results, especially when done strategically. For example, SC Johnson (makers of Johnson Wax) teamed with local organizations and municipalities to create a clear vision for its hometown of Racine, Wisconsin, which was suffering from urban decline. A unique agreement that lowered water and sewer costs for residents was forged among four cities. As the program was implemented, downtown Racine commercial vacancy rates fell from 46 percent to 18 percent. SC Johnson had used its corporate clout to improve the vitality of the community.

SC Johnson contributes 5 percent of its pretax income to such endeavors worldwide, living out its core value: "Every place should be a better place because we are there." In exchange, the company has access to better workers who are proud of their community.

With the Changed Role of Business, Can We Afford to Overlook the Changes in Their Impact on All of Us?

In his book *The Ecology of Commerce*, Paul Hawken said, "Many companies today no longer accept the maxim that the business of business is business. Their new premise is simple: Corporations, because they are the dominant institution on the planet, must squarely address the social and environmental problems that afflict humankind."[25]

Friedman countered this argument: "What it amounts to is an assertion that those who favor the taxes and expenditures in question have failed to persuade a majority of their fellow citizens to be of like mind and that they are seeking to attain by undemocratic procedures what they cannot attain by democratic procedures."[26]

So who is right? Perhaps one way to look at it is to imagine scenarios for each way of addressing the problem. Friedman is asking for the democratic process to produce new laws to address social and economic issues. However, corporations often have a major influence on the shape these laws take. Further, our laws are usually reactionary, responding to problems or scandals. And the scandal cycle keeps repeating itself.

Might not a better alternative be developing corporate consciences that are socially responsible? If the company clearly iterates to shareholders that income will not be produced at the expense of the public interest, we think that Friedman would agree that they are maximizing profits "within the rules of the game, which is to say, engages in open and free competition without deception or fraud."[27] Building on rock means understanding when enough is enough and when other goals are more important than ROI.

Right now, we are experiencing three kinds of sandy ROI:

1. The WorldCom, Enron, Tyco type of fraud where accounting techniques for "smoothing income" slide over the line from creative to illegal.
2. The kind of greed that results in huge profits for executives whether or not the long-term ROI outlook of the corporation is healthy.
3. The burying of the true costs of doing business so that corporate ROI is unaffected by the costs they impose on other parts of society.

There is an alternative. We can re-create the idea that if corporations are going to have the rights of individuals, then they also have the responsibility to be good citizens. Aaron Lamstein, founder of WorldWise, Inc., puts it this way, "Part of our concept is that we must have an incredibly focused mission that includes equally environmental and social issues and economic issues—that is, making sure that we have a really solid, healthy financially secure business."[28]

It isn't either/or. It's both. That's a solid foundation.

DECIDING WHEN ENOUGH IS ENOUGH

Once a business has a vision, the next part of building a solid foundation is determining how that vision influences the level of acceptable profits. Instead of building on the sandy acquiring myth, we can build on rock.

Part of building on the rock is seeing through God's eyes that enough is enough. Remember the following:

- A return on investment is not only moral, but expected.
- God's aim is for everyone to have enough to sustain themselves.
- In determining the profit you can take, the plight of the poor is to be figured in. Some of the harvest goes to them.
- Everything we have comes from God and is to be returned to God.

The other part of the rock is considering the strength of the foundational philosophies. Businesses need a solid foundation to flourish. Malden Mills estimates that it spends several times as much as its competitors do on research and development, ensuring that they continue to make better quality, high-performing products. In contrast, as the market boom continued, more and more dot-coms started on a sandy foundation, without thorough market research. As one businessman put it, "Their business plans were built on the assumption that consumers shared their passion for computers. I'm sorry, but how many hours did they think I wanted to spend in front of my keyboard?"

We've seen what sandy foundations look like: dot-coms or firms such as Enron that were "laser-focused on ROI." Sandy foundations ask that things be done quickly. Strip the topsoil, line your own pockets, work only with people who have the same morals. Sandy companies are all around us—a recent poll revealed that only 63 percent of workers believe their companies conduct their business with honesty and integrity. Only 39 percent trust senior leaders at their firms.[29]

A local newspaper columnist told us that every ten years he ends up writing articles about corporate fraud because the cycle will continue as long as we carry the wrong image of what the companies are for—creating wealth and nothing else. There's a better foundation, one of setting targets for ROI by considering how you will allow it to be created, what you want to do with it, and who can participate in it with you.

Think back to the "home" you created for your corporation in developing a vision. That vision encompasses what will determine the company's ROI. While there is no one correct model, there are questions to ask and principles to keep in mind as you build your model of stewardship, of corporate responsibility, your rock-solid foundation.

Many of the most solid corporations—Johnson & Johnson, 3M, and Nordstrom are a few of the great examples—have already discovered that being stewards of customers, employees, the environment, in short, of all stakeholders, ensures great long-lasting, rock-solid results.

WHY BUILD ON ROCK?

In the summer of 2002, Congress passed the Sarbanes-Oxley Act, aimed at stronger accounting controls, more responsibility for corporate officers, and transparency of financial statements. Just as they had to in the 1980s after the junk bond and savings and loan scandals; just as in the 1930s during the Great Depression. Closing loopholes merely drives the lawyers and accountants and business people to look for new ones.

The new reform measures, while helpful, are so complicated and tangled that even the most sophisticated business person will need legal and accounting advice to ensure compliance. Further, as Patrick Delaney, chair of corporate business at Lindquist & Vennum, points out, "The theory has been sold that transparency in financial records is the highest value, presumably so that investors can see through transactions and thus get to their heart. Anyone who understands the idea of "snowing" someone knows that transparency often generates a blizzard of information that presents an opaque forest rather than identifiable trees."[30]

Merely enacting new accounting changes and corporate governance rules won't fix the fundamental problem that businesses are increasingly complex. Further, as Adam Smith pointed out hundreds of years ago, people will act in their own self-interests unless those interests are curbed by moral guidance.

The stakes for corporate morality, however, have never been higher. Richard Moore, the treasurer for the State of North Carolina, is responsible for over $60 billion in public monies, state investments, and pension funds. He points out that out of the $12 trillion in the market, $2.2 trillion is owned by pension funds; pension funds are the largest clients of mutual funds that control $8 trillion of the market. It follows that in many cases pension funds, collectively, are the largest shareholders of many companies. And they are fiscally responsible for the retirement funds of their clients.

The market downturn wreaked havoc with many of these funds. The ones Moore manages only lost a few percentage points, which has given him credibility to speak for the industry. And, as he puts it,

> What I'm afraid will happen, and this will be catastrophic, is that in the exercise of my fiduciary duty and groups like myself, we will exit this market. . . . You enticed me on to this playing field by telling me it was going to be level. You assure me it's level or I leave. And if I leave, corporate America loses the most efficient means to access capital, which made us the greatest nation on the face of the earth. . . .
>
> And some enterprising person out there is going to say, aha! Why don't we start a new exchange? And I will vouch to you large institutional holders that if you come and play in my game, I'll make sure that there are independent accountants and that there are activists on board. And these are the rules of my game. Now who wants to come join?[31]

The pension funds and the small investors know that the markets don't guarantee any specific return, but they want the markets to be fair. Going back to the biblical text about the homes built on rock and sand, note that Jesus didn't say "If the storms come," but that the rains and storms and winds *came*. About the only certainty of business is that you can't predict the future. However, they want fair markets that aren't prone to the abuses of the dot-com era.

ROCK-SOLID PRINCIPLES

A starting place might be to consider what our society could become if more businesses built on rock. The book of Ezekiel contains an incredible vision of a new temple of the Lord. Ezekiel's account takes us through the gateway, the courts, the priests' rooms, the outer sanctuary with its beautiful carved walls, and the Most Holy Place. At the end of his vision, Ezekiel is taken outside of the temple, where water is flowing out from under the structure. Ezekiel is told,

> When [the river] empties into the Sea, the water there becomes fresh. Swarms of living creatures will live wherever the river flows. There will be large numbers of fish, because this water flows there and makes the salt water fresh; so where the river flows everything will live. Fishermen will stand along the shore; from En Gedi to En Eglaim there will be places for spreading nets. . . . Fruit trees of all kinds will grow on both banks of the river. Their leaves will not wither, nor will their fruit fail. Every month they will bear, because the water from the sanctuary flows to them. Their fruit will serve for food and their leaves for healing.[32]

This temple was never built. Perhaps it is a vision still in our future. What if businesses planned for purpose and profits as God ordained, ensuring that there was enough for everyone and that everything they have really belongs to God? Then corporations could act as a source of life, a river flowing out to water the land. Then businesses return to God's economic model (and incidentally to Adam Smith's) of everyone having enough. This can happen if ROI goals are set in alignment with a business's assignment.

A few years ago, David picked up an Orange County newspaper while he was in California. The front-page picture caught his eye: an entire neighborhood devastated by a mudslide. Only one house was left standing on the hillside.

Curious, David called the newspaper to see if they knew anything about the sole surviving house. "Yes, we do," the editor replied. "It was built by Habitat for Humanity. And, unlike many of the surrounding dwellings, the Habitat people built it to code."

Building on a code for ROI that is sustainable: that's the kind of foundation you want, one that will last through the storms that *will* come.

My father taught me that where there are no people
of moral correctness, I should act as if the entire world
were resting on my shoulders.
—Aaron Feuerstein[33]

TOP-DOWN SOLUTIONS
FOR ROCK-SOLID PROFITS

Rock or sand—individually we seem to know the difference, but corporately the drive for profits often gets in the way. To make the move to ROI, while acknowledging that businesses must remain profitable, we can re-create the idea that if corporations are to have the rights of individuals, they also have the responsibility to be good citizens. The following principles can help you get there.

VALUES BEFORE PROFITS

While profits are essential, companies built on rock know that with the right vision, there is room for values *and* profits.

Honest Tea was founded in 1998. This niche beverage company's mission is to create and promote "great tasting, truly healthy, all-natural beverages made the way their cultures of origin intended. We strive to grow our business with the same honesty and integrity we use to craft our products."[34]

One way the company lives out its mission is by creating partnerships with communities that house their suppliers. They exemplify the biblical principle of ensuring that everyone has enough to sustain themselves. For example, their First Nation Tea is produced through a partnership with the Crow Nation. I'tchik Herb, a woman-owned company based on the Crow reservation, supplies the organic peppermint leaves used in the tea and is an active marketing participant. Royalties are paid to I'tchik and to a nonprofit organization that benefits foster and homeless Native American children.

It took a series of protracted negotiations to develop this partnership, but producing the tea without the approval of Crow tribal elders would have gone against the company's mission. They lived up to their stated social responsibility that "when presented with a purchasing decision between two financially viable alternatives, we will attempt to choose the option that better addresses the needs of economically disadvantaged communities."[35]

The company doubled its sales in 2002 and seems capable of maintaining its stronghold in its niche. "Social Responsibility," says Honest Tea, "is not an excuse for lesser performance by a company."[36]

STAKEHOLDERS AND SHAREHOLDERS

Even though corporate law points to shareholder wealth as the main responsibility of corporate directors, there are many other laws, such as environmental, health, and safety statutes, that must be followed. Again, making a profit is a moral thing to do, but ethics figure into how big that profit can be.

Going back to the stages of law, considering only shareholder wealth is the letter of the law. A company can be on solid legal ground financially without having a corporate calling.

Going a step further, we can look for ways to consider other stakeholders, looking outward to ensure that the golden rule is followed and that we are treating the community, the environment, and employees as we would like to be treated. This sort of attitude often anticipates how laws might evolve. For example, some companies were making "reasonable accommodation" long before the Americans with Disabilities Act mandated that buildings be accessible.

The higher ground, the way of Christ, means that one looks beyond the laws to higher principles altogether. One company that went beyond compliance is FIC Corporation of Rockville, Maryland. This manufacturing firm partnered with a community service organization for people with autism to train and retain their clients as workers. People with autism can become dependable workers, often excelling at repetitive tasks, but each one needs individual coaching to succeed. Further, their coworkers often need to be educated about autism. A coach from the community service organization helps in this role.

The program takes extra effort, but it results in long-term employee retention. In addition, the community saves money since people with disabilities are employed rather than institutionalized. Yet FIC had to go *looking* for the chance to make a difference, to understand what making reasonable accommodation means for workers with autism.

The legal field's current interest in what is known as legal pragmatism reflects the ethical need to look to higher principles. In legal pragmatism, one acknowledges that laws are imperfect and continue to evolve as a democracy redefines values. Public debate of those values comes first and laws follow—society's idea of what is just often evolves, as it did with the Americans with Disabilities Act or environmental issues. Therefore, leaders need to reflect on what the laws might become as they listen to public debate. The advantages of using this interpretation are that:

> pragmatism reminds the manager that the values that underlie law are a product of consensus, not the dictate of a sole conscience, and thereby exhorts the manager to be skeptical of his or her own system of moral law. Second . . . in a pragmatic world, values change and must be evaluated. Third . . . pragmatism promises more flexibility than natural law reasoning, facilitating the balancing of profit with social good.[37]

Somehow, this line of reasoning seems to unite Smith with Friedman in defining the true responsibility of business.

A CULTURE OF TRANSPARENCY

Although transparency can be misused by releasing an avalanche of information to "snow" the reader, its true goal is disclosure.

Financial statements, those documents that present a company's ROI, among other things, are meant to be an accurate picture of business results. However, accounting rules are open to interpretation. Decisions have to be made about asset values, when write-offs should be taken, what might constitute future liabilities, inventory practices, and countless other items.

What we're really talking about is making an accurate measurement of wealth: Is a company measuring its income fairly? Would others agree? In ancient times, fraud was often perpetrated by using different weights to determine the value of crops. Swindlers used one set of weights when buying and another set when selling. God takes this seriously: "You must have accurate and honest weights and measures, so that you may live long in the land the Lord your God is giving you. For the Lord your God detests anyone who does these things, anyone who deals dishonestly."[38]

Honesty and transparency can be subject to different interpretations in complex matters, such as valuing inventory or determining when to take write-offs, but one definition might be that nothing is hidden. Financial statements and footnotes disclose everything the company is aware of. Board members talk not only to top executives, but develop other relationships so they can listen for inconsistencies or silences that might indicate something being kept under wraps. Conflicts of interest are avoided, scrutinized, or otherwise disclosed. Assumptions behind the numbers are stated.

In October 2002, *Standard and Poor's* released a report that showed a marked difference between the market risk of corporations that provided the most extensive disclosure in their annual reports and those who didn't. Areas of disclosure examined included ownership structures, investor rights, and management and board structures and processes, as well as financial data. Those with higher disclosure had higher price-to-book ratios—they were worth more. Their conclusion was that investors should consider transparency and disclosure as a significant measure of risk, along with such standard tools as valuation analysis and credit ratings. The corollary is that corporations can lower the cost of equity capital by providing higher transparency and disclosure. Or, honesty is the best policy.[39]

One corporate controller described it this way: "As soon as you ask, 'Can we do this? Is it legal?' you're on the slippery slope. You're in denial if your only ethical standard is compliance." Part of this truth is the reality that the system provides incentives to highly paid lawyers and accountants to look for ways to hide things. Unless your goal is to be transparent, it's easy to misjudge the line between creative accounting and fraud.

We doubt that many of the financial officers responsible for the most recent round of corporate scandals sat down one day and said, "Let's do fraud." Instead, they took small steps on the slippery slope, which is easy in an acquiring myth culture that hands out bonuses based on statements that, after all, are matters of opinion.

While we hesitate to judge specific companies as transparent, an "opaque" phenomenon appeared in many 2002 corporate annual reports. Inside the shiny covers of many of them was nothing more than a photocopy of the company 10K filing, the bare minimum required by the SEC. No glossy photos, enthusiasm over upcoming plans, or new research and development endeavors. Compliance just doesn't equal transparency.

A COMPENSATION SYSTEM THAT ENCOURAGES "ROCK-SOLID" BEHAVIOR

With bonuses and stock options often based on performance, sometimes those gray areas of accounting practices can make a difference of millions of dollars to those who are making the financial decisions—including board members who are charged with the responsibility of reviewing the statements. When bonuses are given at certain earnings levels, the pressure increases to massage profits over the target level—or, if the numbers aren't close, to pull losses that may hit the next quarter into the current quarter to have a better chance at a bigger bonus the next time around. This turns accounting into a game rather than a communication of results.

Also problematic is the way bonus systems have led to huge disparities between executives and sales or marketing personnel versus the rest of a company. The net result is a corporate aristocracy that is far-removed from everyday people. A factory floor employee put this better than we can: "Every time my company announces that there are good earnings or higher profits, it's because of management's strategy and plans, and they get multimillion dollar bonuses. But every time our profits and earnings have gone down, it's because of foreign competition, and workers are fired and bonuses are cut on the working people down the line."[40]

Companies who want compensation to drive desired behavior often have to make adjustments after a system is implemented. For example, one retailer experimented with different ways of giving bonuses to all employees of stores that exceeded projected earnings. They learned that store results were better if store managers received a bonus based on exceeding projections—giving equal bonuses to everyone simply wasn't as effective. However, when everyone shared in savings that came from reducing theft, shoplifting was reduced.

AES, an independent energy producer, ties executive bonuses not just to financial performance but to technical factors such as safety records, community relations, and environmental data as well as adherence to the corporation's values of integrity, fairness, fun, and social responsibility. In 1998, bonuses were cut due to four fatal accidents. Their overall safety ratings remained well above industry averages, yet the cuts were made in recognition of the tragedies.

Other companies have increased productivity throughout the system by giving bonuses based on profits to everyone who is performing at least satisfactorily, from the CEO to the newest receptionist. While employees certainly shouldn't feel entitled to bonuses if either personal or overall corporate performance falls short, the principle of everyone having enough should be a check on runaway bonuses for people at the top.

Remember, profits are to be laid back at the feet of the one who created us. Part of this stewardship is ensuring that the profits were shared. The sharing doesn't have to be equal, but everyone is to have enough.

A CULTURE OF TRUTHFULNESS, ACCOUNTABILITY, AND WITH ROOM FOR DIFFERENCE OF OPINION

Fairness in compensation, willingness to own up to mistakes, and respect for those who question decisions all have to start at the top. Consider the promise Ron Jensen made when he was director of public works for the city of Phoenix, Arizona, to publish *all* questions that employees submitted to question boxes he placed throughout his organization. He guaranteed that he wouldn't edit them (other than for obscenities) and would answer them as honestly as he could.

At first the few letters placed in the boxes were either attacks on Ron himself or hostile notes, reflecting the turmoil the two-thousand-person department was in when he took over. However, when workers saw that even these letters were being published, they started submitting serious questions, so many that Jensen tripled the size of the newsletter. Soon, suggestions and ideas to improve the many inefficiencies and problems were mixed in with the questions. The department's turnaround was so remarkable that it was featured in a PBS documentary *Promoting the Common Good—Excellence in the Public Sector.*

A PLAN FOR GROWTH OVER TIME RATHER THAN BIG BREAKTHROUGHS

The opportunists of the dot-com era were looking for the one big chance. Often, they weren't building anything, but instead were looking for a way to flip. The founders of E-Loan, though, looked at it differently. The founder of this Web-based mortgage company meant to streamline things for the consumer, Janina Pawlowski, said, "We wanted to build something sustainable, something big, something that would change an industry that wasn't working." Like many of the other dot-coms, they worked their tails off to prove that the business could work, but Janina refused to sell when Intuit tried to buy E-Loan after two years for $130 million. She didn't want to give up her dream that "if we did all types of debt really well, and did them worldwide, then E-Loan would become a much stronger company than Countrywide, for example, or Norwest."

Instead, she found new investors, including Yahoo! so she could continue to work on her dream. Rating systems place them as the number-one online brand. Company president Joe Kennedy says, "Sure, speed matters: Whenever we see an opportunity to improve our Web site, we want to capitalize on that opportunity in two weeks or less. But we are also developing an organization—and again that takes time, consistency, and constancy."[41]

Planning for the long term often covers all five stewardships, for corporations who plan on existing into the future care about profits and purpose, people, products, and our planet.

Planning for the short term, building on sand looks like renegade Han Solo in the middle of the first *Star Wars* movie when he tells Princess Leia that he will help her if he is well paid, since he's in it for the money. Her reply is to the point: "If money is all that you love, then that's what you'll receive."

It's the choice each of us faces as we choose between return on investment or return on integrity.

BOTTOM-UP STRATEGIES FOR ROCK-SOLID PROFITS

Achieving inner contentment: not to have what we want but rather to want and appreciate what we have.
—The Dalai Lama[42]

Tackling the issues surrounding corporate profits and corporate responsibility seems futile, given their enormity and the global implications. If you work for a small company, it may seem as if your firm has little or no impact on them. And, if you work for a multinational, it may seem as if you can have no impact on your firm!

One of the tools for influence is being aware of the questions you can use to determine whether an ROI is also a return on integrity. We used the following case study with a group of modern business people. "What if you were offered two investments? One would provide an annual return of 33 percent and the other of 50 percent. Which would you choose?"

This group had been part of our conversations about corporate calling. All were people of integrity who were working on their calling long before they met us. Assuming that there was some trick to our question, they grilled us with the following questions:

• What is the nature of the companies, the key players and their experience levels?
• Do I understand and believe in their product? Does it abuse the planet?

- Who are their competitors? What other market details should we know?
- Would I be comfortable telling my minister that I made that much money on this investment?
- What's the risk-adjusted return? How likely am I to see the profits?
- Why can't the lower one make 50 percent as well?

Their questions were right on target, and the first few were similar to questions that the authorities asked almost four hundred years ago when Boston businessman Robert Keaynes was brought to trial for making the usurious returns of 33 to 50 percent on his business of selling bags of nails, buttons, and thread. Keaynes claimed that he was innocent; he had worked hard for his money and his fellow Puritans were mistaking industry for greed. He considered himself a good Christian and hadn't charged more than the market would bear.

However, Keaynes operated within a system that insisted that business people must be stewards of whatever they accumulated, using wealth for righteous purposes if they dared accumulate it in the first place. He was convicted of greed and corrupt business practices. First the civil courts fined him. Then the Church declared he had to publicly acknowledge his sins or be excommunicated.

MAKING IT PERSONAL

Would any of us consider Keaynes out of line today, especially if his business gave satisfactory answers to the questions our group of businesspeople raised? Before we can tackle corporate greed, it might be a good idea to look hard at our own desires. For example, Jamal is a police officer. His wife Susan is a schoolteacher. Are they rich? Are you rich?

If Jamal and Susan's salaries are average for their professions, together they gross more than 75 percent of the other households in the United States. That's right, in the year 2000, a household income greater than $55,000 put Jamal and Susan in the top 25 percent. They may even be in the top 10 percent, making over $92,000.[43] So would a two-income couple where both are union assembly-line workers, or an experienced nurse and a senior pastor at a mid-sized church. If asked, however, none of these people would say they're in the upper income brackets.

Almost no one in America says they are. In fact, research shows that no matter what income or net-worth bracket people are in, they believe that "rich" people make or have double what they do.[44] What we earn isn't enough—and we see ourselves as much less well-off in comparison to others than we really are.

The Bible tells us that the love of money, not money itself, is the root of all evil. On the pragmatic side, the preacher of Ecclesiastes reminds us of how futile building bigger barns becomes: "For to the one who pleases him, God gives wisdom and knowledge and joy; but to the sinner he gives the work of gathering and heaping, only to give to one who pleases God. This also is vanity and a chasing after wind."[45]

Knowing that we are chronically dissatisfied with what we have—in the words of the Dalai Lama, not appreciating what we have—is perhaps the first step toward acknowledging that our own outlook is entwined in the acquiring myth. Being content with what we have might mean:

- Remembering that in the 1950s, a home with 950 square feet was the norm. The average new garage is bigger than that. Our present home may be big enough.[46]
- Remembering that a household income greater than $28,000 is higher than 50 percent of the households in the United States.[47]
- Remembering that much of the rest of the world cannot imagine closets full of clothes, even if we think they are out of fashion. Or owning a car, let alone having more than one per licensed driver, as we now have in the United States.

On the other hand, as Aaron Feuerstein of Malden Mills pointed out, the Bible makes clear that businesses are not supposed to take advantage of their workers. We can ask for fair pay and that profits not be made at our expense. Yet until we own up to how the acquiring myth affects us personally, it can keep us from questioning a company's profit motives, incentive plans, earnings sources, and expense levels.

Looking for employment at nonprofit organizations is not the only solution. Every company needs reminders of how to keep from just building bigger barns, of how to build on a foundation of pure rock. And each of us is only responsible to wield the influence we can with the power we have, be it great or small.

ROI, without the solid foundation, becomes a chasing after wind. If you truly believe that every number going into an earnings statement is as important as the bottom line, then you might look for ways to move toward an ROI that would be more productive for everyone—a return on integrity rather than just on investment.

A RETURN ON INTEGRITY

If you do not own a business or are not a higher-level manager, there are still ways to influence ROI. Here are a few strategies to try.

Show the Savings

Try showing the benefits of the new ROI (Return on Integrity); for example, in a typical corporate budget process. Departments often pad their expense estimates, lessening the chance that they will go over budget. Those responsible for allocations know about the padding, so they make cuts. Adding to the confusion, at the end of the year, if a department hasn't spent as much as was allocated to them, the managers feel compelled to make purchases to avoid getting less money the next year. Not only do people not tell the truth, they know that everyone else is hiding information as well.

Think of how much time would be saved if the budget game stopped, if everyone turned in honest estimates and returned unused funds—once again, a true return on integrity.

Unearth the Evidence

More and more companies are starting to consider values as well as profits. Scan the news and the Internet for examples that your company can relate to. For example, evidence exists that honesty *is* the best policy to maximize profits. In 1991, Carmax surveyed its customers and quickly discovered that people equated buying used cars with a trip to the dentist for a root canal. In response, Carmax incorporated as normal business procedures things like stating fair prices immediately, providing limited warranties, and fully disclosing reconditioning work. They quickly became one of the largest used car dealers in the company—and their Web site reports that 97 percent of their customers would recommend Carmax to a friend.

Grab the Brass Ring

Check out company policies. If they offer paid time for volunteer work, use it and encourage those around you to do the same. If they will donate supplies to schools or nonprofit organizations, tell people you know in those fields all about it. If you can, sponsor a youth sports team, provide a free meeting room to a just-forming community action group, bring a meal to Habitat for Humanity workers, or any other service.

Timberland, a U.S. manufacturer of boots and shoes, includes a generous program for employees to take time off for volunteer activities. In addition, there are company-wide community service days. Over the years, Timberland has seen this program foster loyalty in its own employees.

In other words, make the most of any beginnings your company has toward a return on integrity, not just on investment. Then document what happens.

Lay Out the Scenarios

All financial planning is a gamble; no one can predict the future. Scenario planning is one way of dealing with uncertainty. Instead of basing strategic plans on what you believe to be the most likely future, lay out several likely scenarios. Whereas most strategic planning focuses on honing the best assumptions, scenario planning begins by asking critical questions that unearth different plausible sets of assumptions. Then, large projects are considered in the context of each of these scenarios about the future. Plans are measured in terms of how well they fare in very different future scenarios, not just in what the players assume to be the most likely future.

Shell used this strategy to think about worldwide oil reserve consumption. One of their scenarios involved what would happen if governments restricted the flow of oil, even though this seemed unlikely back in the 1960s. Because their strategy had considered the appearance of what came to be OPEC, Shell weathered the ensuing oil crisis better than the other major oil companies.

While all of these things may seem like nothing more than gnats biting at the corporate ROI elephant, when too many insects gather, an elephant heads for the nearest water hole to spray away the pests. Further, remember that when we start asking "How?" too soon we're rushing past the question of whether we're doing the right thing. Encouraging a corporation to consider whether their ROI is being generated at the expense of employees, customers, the community, or the environment is the right thing to do.

WHERE SHOULD THE PURSUIT OF PROFITS STOP?

It may be that neither your company nor those around you have the slightest hint that they are building on sand instead of rock. The acquiring myth can look like the thing to do: Get stable financially *before* thinking about good works or good employee benefits or a balanced life.

Sensational examples, such as Enron, illustrate starkly how corporations can go wrong in the all-out pursuit of profits, but few of us have the opportunities for greed that its fallen executives encountered.

If you think that the business of business needs to remain business, take a look at the practices of the company *Fortune Magazine* bills as the only company Wal-Mart fears: Costco. CEO Jim Sinegal continues to run Costco according to four basic principles:

- *Obey the law.* They strictly adhere to health and safety regulations as well as above-board dealings with buyers and suppliers.
- *Take care of your customers.* Mark-ups are never more than 14 percent. Period. They may run as high as 40 percent at department stores. The founder, Sol Price, said, "You are the fiduciary of the customer. You've got to give before you get. If you get something for a lower price, you pass on the savings." Their return policy is still no receipts, no questions, no time limits except for a six-month window on computers.
- *Take care of your employees.* Retail employees start at $10 per hour, the highest of any chain. Employee salaries reach $40,000 after four years. Their benefits are generous. Sinegal's own salary for 2002 was only $350,000, low by corporate standards; further, he's capped his salary and bonus at twice the level of his store managers.
- *Practice the intelligent loss of sales.* Costco continues to streamline product choices. While some customers may

refuse to purchase substitutes for favorite brands, most don't mind, and the savings in distribution and inventory costs make up for lost sales.

With these as a foundation, Costco experiences an employee turnover rate that is only a third the rate of other retailers. The rate of employee theft is only 13 percent of the industry as a whole. While they have 29 percent fewer stores than Sam's Club, their major competitor, their sales were 5 percent higher and the average Costco store generates nearly double the revenue of a Sam's Club store. The strategies work.

Yet those strategies bring down the wrath of Wall Street. Analysts consistently cry for lower labor costs. Deutsche Bank analyst Bill Dreher complained, "Costco continues to be a company that is better at serving the club member and employee than the shareholder."

Sinegal counters, "We think when you take care of your customer and your employees, your shareholders are going to be rewarded in the long run . . . we're not going to do something for the sake of one quarter that's going to destroy the fabric of our company and what we stand for."[48]

Consider the kind of return on integrity your company is producing:

• Are people able to bring values, such as honesty and integrity, to the workplace?
• Are dreams and ideas that tie to stewardship nurtured or are they sacrificed in the name of profit?
• Are lessons from the past considered in decisions?

What about the atmosphere of your workplace?

• Do employees enjoy work and each other?
• Is there time for family and friends?
• Is the company part of a community or is it an island unto itself?

Finally, what kind of a legacy is your company building?

- Would stakeholders be saddened if the company no longer existed?
- Are memorable contributions, in terms of innovation, service, or ideas, being created?
- Has the company created enemies that would gladly watch its downfall?

Enron doesn't stack up very well, nor does WorldCom or the plethora of companies that disappeared when the bull market of the 1990s went south. Executives from Enron and WorldCom cashed in on stock options but face criminal charges. For WorldCom's former CFO Sullivan, it's up to sixty-five years in prison.

It's a thought for every business and a thought for each one of us. Are we building on sand or rock?

For where your treasure is, there your heart will be also.
 —Matthew 6:21 (NIV)

CHAPTER 5

PRODUCTS AND PLACES

THE GREAT GLOBAL PIE-EATING CONTEST

The earth was made for Dombey and Son to trade in,
and the sun and moon were made to give them light.
Rivers and seas were formed to float their ships;
rainbows gave them promise of fair weather;
winds blew for or against their enterprises;
stars and planets circled in their orbits,
to preserve inviolate a system of which they were the center.
    —Charles Dickens, *Dombey and Son*

IF YOU THINK THAT DICKENS WAS EXAGGERATING, THAT NO corporation truly believes that the earth was made for them, consider one industry's impact on one little corner of the world: "four deaths a day."

That was the estimate the Mexican Ministry of Health gave for fatal pesticide poisonings in 1993. That was the year Anita Roddick, founder of The Body Shop, spent two weeks touring the Nayarit coast tobacco plantations where Huichol Indians worked as day laborers.

Descendents of the Aztecs, the Huichols had lived for centuries in the rugged Sierra Madras, growing corn and hunting in the thick forests. But in 1976, timber companies began constructing roads to harvest the virgin timber. With game growing sparse and the delicate ecobalance needed for mountainside agriculture disrupted, the Huichols had few options other than migrant farm work.

In the makeshift villages along the tobacco fields, Anita saw firsthand the rampant birth defects among the Huichol; her heart sickened at the number of babies being born without genitalia. The workers, both adults and children (families work together since wages are based on the amount of work performed), showed high rates of cancer, blood diseases, and disorders of the immune and nervous systems. It wasn't uncommon for workers to die suddenly as they moved among the tobacco plants.

Scientists knew the cause: the pesticides workers used in the tobacco fields. Long since banned in many other countries, workers were to apply them only while wearing masks, gloves, and protective clothing. The Huichols had none. Some of the chemicals can kill a man if only a few drops are ingested. The overseers urged frequent applications, usually at the request of tobacco companies. Little effort was made to train the workers to use them properly, nor was any care taken to minimize harm to the environment.[1]

Anita learned that while American tobacco companies purchased the crops from these fields, they claimed no responsibility for the misuse of pesticides because they did not own the fields. Their attitude smacked of imperialism. Few people want to admit that America might have imperialist tendencies, pointing to our lack of colonization. However, look at the definition of imperialism: extending the power and dominion of a nation by gaining indirect control over the political or economic life of other areas. Just like *Dombey and Son*, which Dickens brought to life at the height of the Age of Imperialism, the tobacco companies acted as if the sun and the moon were made to give them light.

Outraged, Anita used photos and tales of the peasant farm workers' plight as the focus of a speech she gave to the International Chamber of Commerce meeting in Cancun just two weeks after her stay with the Huichols. The reaction of these leaders in world business? Anita said:

I don't quite know what response I expected. I thought there would be some reaction, even if they howled me off the stage. But there was absolutely none—no embarrassment, no sense of outrage, just a collegiate sense of good manners. . . . If business comes with no moral sympathy or honourable code of behaviour, then God help us all."[2]

Are companies truly operating without moral sympathy? Anita's audience was filled with business leaders from a wide range of industries, not just tobacco, all seemingly indifferent to the command to "stop oppressing those who work for you. Treat them fairly and give them what they earn."[3]

Their indifference is formed amidst the economic wisdom of our time, which claims that globalization is good for all players. Corporate and governmental policies alike espouse that free trade and investment, without tariffs or other barriers, create jobs and increase available markets for every country involved.

If this is so, then why did at least seventy-five thousand people block the streets of Seattle in protest of the 1999 meetings of the World Trade Association (WTO)? Why did thousands of people demonstrate in Washington, D.C., against the International Monetary Fund (IMF) and World Bank during their April 2000 meetings? Why did crowds of over one hundred thousand gather in Genoa, Italy, in the summer of 2001?

Perhaps you've seen pictures of protestors who seemed more radical than a millennium cult, but is that sensationalism or balanced reporting? Who is right? The protestors or the IMF and WTO? Anita Roddick was on the front lines in Seattle, handing out fruit and nuts to the protestors who successfully delayed the meetings' start by several hours. She said,

I think about how relentless the protesters are. Day after day, no matter what the authorities and the police throw at them, they keep on coming back. . . . They seem determined to create a world where reverence is what we practise [sic], with work that fulfils us, building communities based on interdependence and co-operation and nurturing relationships that breathe passion into our lives.

But I also wonder whether I have had a real-life glimpse of what corporate-controlled reality looks like: police in the streets, no civil rights, martial law, and jail brutality.[4]

How much is she exaggerating? So that you can judge for yourself, let's look first at the *intent* of corporate policies and then the *results* of those policies.

To understand whether corporations still believe that "rivers and seas were formed to float their ships," we performed a cursory review of the 2001 annual reports of major multinational firms. Actually, we stopped after only three—Coca-Cola, General Electric, and General Motors—for each showed a resemblance to Dombey & Son:

> Through innovative marketing programs, we deepened the already strong connections between consumers and the world's most popular brand, reminding them of why they trust us to deliver refreshment anytime, anywhere—from New York to Shanghai. . . .

> We will manufacture CT scanners in China and side-by-side refrigerators in Mexico, and we will provide administrative services and software from India—all with higher quality and lower costs. . . . We see globalization from multiple angles. We support our customers everywhere in the world.

> We will maintain our momentum in 2002 by continuing to focus on increasing our market share in all our markets around the globe, on progressing toward industry leadership in quality and productivity, and on creating innovative, head-turning cars and trucks. . . .

None of these statements are inherently bad; we present these quotes from their 2001 letters to shareholders only to demonstrate that increasing world market share is key to the corporate strategies of Coca-Cola, General Electric, and General Motors, and other multinational firms. That is their intent. And it's what their shareholders expect; market growth drives increasing ROI. The question is, what is the impact of their ever-increasing drive for market share?

Market share is often depicted as a slice on a pie chart—with each market player vying for the largest slice of the pie. You might even refer to globalization as a great, worldwide pie-eating contest. And in contests, there are winners and losers.

The losers of the global pie-eating contest are getting tired of eating nothing but crumbs, but they're having a hard time being heard. Listen and look closely, though, and you can hear their grievances.

THE RESULTS OF CORPORATE INTENT

For a moment, picture yourself as a villager in the Niger Delta of Nigeria. There is no running water, no electricity, not even a school in the village. Vast reserves of oil exist under the paths you walk each day between the village well and the hut where you live. But the oil is owned by ChevronTexaco, not Nigeria. The oil workers in a nearby export facility have a modern hospital, satellite TV, and nice homes, while you can barely scrape out a living.

In the summer of 2002, six hundred village women staged a nonviolent takeover of the Escravos export facility, demanding work for their sons and the help of ChevronTexaco in making improvements in their village. Over seven hundred oil workers were held hostage for ten days while the women negotiated with an executive. Before the protest ended, the executive had signed an agreement to:

- Employ twenty-five villagers over the next five years and make the fifteen currently employed permanent instead of temporary employees.
- Install electricity and water systems in local villages.
- Build schools, clinics, and town halls.
- Help build fish and chicken farms so that villagers can raise and sell food to the oil facilities.

As the women released the hostages, the executive said, "We now have a different philosophy, and that is to do more with communities." As word of the victory spread, four more oil facilities in the area were seized by other groups of women.[5]

While this might sound like progress, it's also a case of too little, very late. One would think that the oil company's philosophy had already had plenty of reason to change, given what has happened in the country. Since 1975, Nigeria's per capita income has dropped by 23 percent, despite $300 billion earned from oil. The pattern has been repeated in Chad, Gabon, Algeria—all over the world. The oil money goes to a corrupt few, the promise of easy wealth leads to political conflict, and leaders who might otherwise invest in their people instead fight for their share of the profits. In the meantime, the poor grow poorer as development pushes up the local costs for food, clothing, and shelter.

But these injustices pale in comparison to the events of 1995, when eight leaders of another Nigerian people, the Ogoni, were hanged on trumped-up charges. The dictatorship government which then ruled Nigeria performed the executions to silence the Ogoni protests against Shell Oil's environmental impact and lack of economic justice. After all that, it took the women's protest for ChevronTexaco to say, "We now have a different philosophy, and that is to do more with communities."

What does a corporation like ChevronTexaco truly owe to the villagers? They're covering all of the oil extraction costs and containing their activities to a small area. The villagers lack the education to perform all but a handful of jobs at the oil facilities. What is just?

These aren't easy questions and alternative answers abound, depending on your perspective. What if, for example, you had the perspective of someone in charge of the oil company *and* the villagers? Your viewpoint might be as follows:

The sun still drifted low in the eastern sky as the shepherd guided his flock into a new pasture, just over the hill from their old grazing spot. Tiny rainbows of dew shimmered in the early morning daylight, making the grass look as inviting as the grandest banquet table.

Maybe this time will be different, thought the shepherd. *There's plenty of food for all—and the stream is clear and long so that all of the animals can get to the water, unlike the old mud hole.* He looked at some of the smaller animals that had struggled for every mouthful of grass in the old pasture. There, a few of the larger animals had charged to the best grazing spots every morning. They'd eaten so much that they could barely stagger away for a drink of water. And, while they left handfuls of grass behind, the way they pushed and butted the others away trampled the remaining blades of nourishment into the mud.

The shepherd sighed. How could he make sure the weaklings in the flock got enough?[6]

Ezekiel used this image of the fat sheep trampling the grass to speak to the Israelites of the injustices he saw and to warn them that God would rescue the lean sheep and judge the fat ones. The ChevronTexaco executive is just beginning to grapple with reality as demonstrated throughout history: Eventually, the lean sheep get tired of muddy grass. The fat sheep can continue to spend millions on security, trying to keep their huge slice of the pie, or they can put their efforts into working with those around them.

GLOBALIZATION: THE WORLDWIDE PIE-EATING CONTEST

There are a lot of big, fat sheep in the world today. Globalization means that corporations have more places to increase market share. If product sales stagnate in the United States, it's time to introduce it in overseas markets. It's a byproduct of the acquiring myth: A saturated market is no excuse for lack of revenue growth. Instead, one has to find a bigger pie to bite into. Thus begins the worldwide pie-eating contest.

Listen to the language of one company: "[W]e expect the weak economic conditions in many Asian and Latin American markets to continue for some time. Yet, these countries represent an enormous long-term opportunity for McDonald's, given their potential for economic growth and their large populations."[7] We aren't picking on McDonald's; we could have picked almost any global corporation. Market forces view international markets as a contest to see who can grab the biggest slice of the pie. The winners get fatter while the losers struggle to find a way to compete at all in a world stacked against them.

Our government, the media, and corporations assure us that to avoid the pie-eating contest, to ensure that all the sheep have a chance to feast on the global grasses, we must work harder than ever to make free trade among nations a reality. Behind the design of the World Trade Organization, the drive for our president to be able to negotiate trade agreements independently, and sweeping legislation such as the General Agreement on Tariffs and Trade (GATT) or the North American Free Trade Agreement (NAFTA) is this core ideology:

> Economic globalization, achieved by removing barriers to the free flow of goods and money anywhere in the world, spurs competition, increases economic efficiency, creates jobs, lowers consumer prices, increases consumer choice, increases economic growth, and is generally beneficial to almost everyone.[8]

This ideology is based firmly on the current ruling model of macroeconomics. The IMF claims that the number of people living on less than $2 a day (in 1985 dollars) has fallen from 38 percent to 19 percent in the twenty years ended in 1998,[9] but that says nothing about buying power—and one of the effects of development is increased prices for food and housing. They claim that health and safety requirements increase the cost of goods, but might health and safety be worth the price increases? They say that trade results in better infrastructure, phones, roads, and power, but as the women of the Niger Delta will testify, that may not help the poor. And even the IMF admits that "there is no systematic relationship between openness [of trade] and the income of the poorest."[10]

A quick search of news headlines published in the four weeks before the Washington, D.C., protests against the IMF in September 2002 shows some of the results of "free trade" funded by the IMF or World Bank:

- *Columbia Leader Says Trying to Avoid Economic Ruin—* "Columbia's President Alvaro Uribe called on his war-torn nation and the world to help him rescue the economy on Sunday, imploring citizens to support tax hikes and budget cuts while asking global lenders for cash."[11]
- *Paraguay Bottlenecked in New Anti-Government Protest—* "Trucks and tractors parked up on highways at intervals and protesting taxi drivers caused havoc with a go-slow in the capital Asuncion to decry government price hikes and plans to up taxes they say are prolonging a crushing seven-year recession."[12]

- *U.S. Envoy Sounds Out Brazilian Candidates' Policies*—"The opposition candidates' lead has scared many U.S. investors, who fear an opposition victory could mean a rollback of market-friendly policies."[13]

The protests come because the economic development supported by proponents of free markets—also known as the pie-eating contest—doesn't help the people who live in the countries. David Korten, author of *When Corporations Rule the World,* put it this way:

> This kind of growth requires gearing the economy toward exports to earn foreign exchange to buy the things that wealthy people desire. Thus the lands of the poor are appropriated for export crops. The former tillers of these lands then find themselves subsisting in urban slums on starvation wages paid by sweatshops producing items for export. Families are broken up, the social fabric is strained to the breaking point, and violence becomes endemic. Those whom growth has favored then need still more foreign exchange to import arms to protect themselves from the rage of the excluded.[14]

Could it be that the protestors, usually portrayed in the press by the more radical actions of a few people, are right about the impact of free trade? Is it trampling the hungry sheep?

THE WORLD OF MACROECONOMICS

Free trade is a sacred ideology for many economists, but let's step for a moment into their world. Economics is generally referred to as a social science. In science, you put forth theories and then use the scientific method to test how well they describe reality. In doing so you have to make certain assumptions or place some restrictions on the conditions under which a theory holds true. For example, a feather will fall faster in a vacuum, unaffected by gravity and air flow, than in the real world. These assumptions are explicit. Remember taking physics tests? *Calculate the speed at which this object will travel down this inclined plane. Assume there is no friction.* Adding friction to the calculation completely changes the equation—and the answer. The difference can be life or death if you're using these theories to construct bridges or buildings.

Macroeconomics works the same way: Economists build models that take into account certain assumptions about reality. Unlike physics, however, the models cannot be tested in laboratories; they get tested in real economies—with results like the village women in Nigeria protesting that "economic growth" in the region left them poorer than before their way of life was disturbed.

Consider the above ideology used to advocate for global free trade. Here is a sample of the assumptions underlying the model that Congress relied on in passing the legislation that enacted NAFTA in 1994:

- *Capital is immobile. Therefore companies can't move manufacturing plants to other countries.*
  False; even before NAFTA, major American companies were already employing half a million Mexican workers just over that country's border.
- *Unit labor costs are the same in different countries.*
  False; average manufacturing wages in the United States are much higher than in Mexico.
- *Americans clearly prefer American-made products and will pay a premium for them over foreign goods.*
  False; for the auto industry alone, by 1994, 24 percent[15] of cars driven in America were purchased overseas.
- *North American countries are experiencing full employment.*
  False; the unemployment rate in the United States was 6.1 percent and in Mexico it hovered between 14 to 17 percent in 1994.[16]
- *Exports and imports between countries will be balanced.*
  False; the wages of Mexican workers aren't high enough to send them to superstores to purchase the latest in American consumer goods.

These assumptions aren't merely preposterous, they were known to be preposterous at the time. Consider the following analogy:

If an engineer built a bridge without taking into consideration such realities as the effect of winds, earthquakes, gravity, and traffic, the unlucky people driving across it as it collapsed would have the right to sue. And even those who are tired of the escalation of frivolous lawsuits would agree that the suit was justified. Negligence, pure and simple.

But when economic assumptions displace indigenous peoples, eliminate jobs, hurt the environment, or impose cultural changes, our laws say it is justified in the name of economic growth.

WHOA!

If you haven't been made aware of this before, you may be wondering if we are on the fringe, demonstrating in the streets against globalization. If this describes your reaction, we encourage you to consider the following:

- The passage of NAFTA was backed by the Business Roundtable which created a "front" organization, USA*NAFTA to provide "Americans with assurances through editorials, op-ed pieces, news releases, and radio and television commentaries that NAFTA would provide them with high-paying jobs, stop immigration from Mexico, and raise environmental standards."[17]
- *The New York Times* performed the "public service" of publishing a front-page primer on trade economics so the public would understand the benefits of NAFTA. None of the above assumptions were mentioned, nor were letters to the editor written by experts who opposed NAFTA ever published.
- *When Corporations Rule the World,* which helped open our eyes to the globalization crisis, was written by Dr. David C. Korten, who has an MBA and PhD from Stanford. He served in Vietnam, then joined the faculty of the Harvard School of Business, then moved to the Harvard Institute for International Development. He spent fifteen years in Asia working with the U.S. Agency for International Development. While there he became convinced that U.S. policies were creating the very problems they meant to solve in foreign countries. Archbishop Desmond Tutu said of

When Corporations Rule the World, "This is a 'must read' book—a searing indictment of an unjust international economic order, not by a wild-eyed idealistic left-winger, but by a sober scion of the establishment with impeccable credentials."

We don't know all of the fallout from globalization because the media aren't telling us. Democracy does not work, as educator and philosopher John Dewey reminded us, when big business controls "the means of production, exchange, publicity, transportation and communication, reinforced by command of the press, press agents and other means of publicity and propaganda."[18] Instead of democracy, one might say we have a "corporatocracy."

Mergers and acquisitions have created some immense fat sheep in the news business. Remember, six firms dominate American mass media: General Electric (NBC), Disney (ABC), Viacom (CBS), Bertelsmann (largest book publisher), AOL Time Warner, and Rupert Murdoch's News Corp. (FOX, newspapers, magazines). They have bigger annual revenues than the next twenty firms combined. And they influence the news we see. For example, by 1998, the amount of foreign news reported by the major networks was only half the amount shown in the 1980s. Peter Arnett, a veteran foreign correspondent, said, "I'll put it simply: International news coverage in most of America's mainstream papers has almost reached the vanishing point. Today, a foreign story that doesn't involve bombs, natural disasters, or financial calamity has little chance of entering the American consciousness. . . ."[19]

In essence, most of us didn't hear about the eight Ogoni tribesmen hung in 1995 because the American media downplayed the story. *Censored 1997: The News That Didn't Make the News*[20] listed it as one of the top twenty-five underreported stories of the year. Amnesty International tried to make U.S. citizens aware of the tragedy by placing advertisements about the Ogoni in the Houston papers (where Shell Oil is based), but the ads were rejected.

Further, remember that the government that is advocating free markets was elected in campaigns where the richest one-quarter of one percent of Americans made 80 percent of all individual political contributions and where corporations outspent labor unions ten to one. It makes sense because political contributions become investments in keeping the rules of the game in favor of big business.

Our biggest corporations are winning the pie-eating contest. Slowly but surely since the founding of our country, power has shifted from democracy, as defined by "one person, one vote," to corporations that were originally to serve the common good. Perhaps our wisest president, Abraham Lincoln, said it best when he observed this trend a century and a half ago:

> Corporations have been enthroned . . . an era of corruption in high places will follow and the money power will endeavor to prolong its reign by working on the prejudices of the people . . . until wealth is aggregated in a few hands . . . and the Republic is destroyed.[21]

We've started to unearth what the acquiring myth has kept America from realizing: We are becoming the big, fat sheep of the world. And as we grow fatter, not only are we keeping others from their fair share, but we are trampling all the grass. Soon we too will be on the losing side of the great global pie-eating contest.

CHANGING ORTHODOXY:
ASSESSING THE EXPENSE OF FREE TRADE

The free trade pie-eating contest may be the orthodox economic view, but just because something is the orthodox view doesn't mean it's right. Think back to dessert time around the dining room table. "I get to cut the pie," one of your siblings shouted. But then Mother said, "Go ahead, dear, but the person who slices the pie gets last choice of servings." Silence. Not because of disappointment, but because of the cutter's intense concentration on making every piece equal.

With trade, God doesn't insist that everyone's share be equal, but that everyone has enough. Remember our definition of economic justice:

• A return on investment is not only moral, but expected.
• God's aim is for everyone to have enough to sustain themselves.

- In determining profits, the plight of the poor is to be considered.
- Everything we have comes from God and is to be laid back at the feet of the master.

If we aren't cutting up the pie with that in mind, the prophet Ezekiel makes it crystal clear what will happen to the fat sheep who continue to monopolize the pastures (and eat all the pie):

> For you fat sheep push and butt and crowd my sick and hungry flock until they are scattered to distant lands. So I will rescue my flock, and they will no longer be abused and destroyed. And I will judge between one sheep and another.[22]

Eventually, justice catches up with the pie-eaters. We can wait for it to happen or we can work to change the orthodoxy that claims that free markets are free when they aren't.

Challenges to orthodoxy take years to sort out, but truth eventually triumphs. Six hundred years ago, many of Columbus's contemporaries thought he was going to sail right off the edge of our very flat world. For centuries, chemists recognized only the four elements of earth, fire, air, and water. More recently in 1928, a symposium attended by the leading geologists of the day dismissed the theory of continental drift and plate tectonics "once and for all" (their once and for all lasted twenty-five years). Their reasoning? No natural forces were strong enough to cause such movement.

The notion of free markets, internationally, is an orthodoxy that needs to be subjected to the light of truth. The success of free markets depends in part on having a level playing field as well as a belief in the forces that cause markets to return to equilibrium, that is, that changes in product supply and consumer demand, pricing, wages, and so forth, will eventually stabilize in an optimal way. One by one, these orthodoxies need to be buried if the great global pie-eating contest is to be ended before there is no pie left for anyone.

Free Markets Do Not Move toward Equilibrium
In truth, the acquiring myth fuels the world's markets, just as it does so many of us individually. In *The Crisis of Global Capitalism*, George Soros, who is a leading investment fund manager and who

understood the market well enough to become a billionaire through what some have called manipulation, says, "Capitalism needs democracy as a counterweight because the capitalist system by itself shows no tendency toward equilibrium. The owners of capital seek to maximize their profits. Left to their own devices, they would continue to accumulate capital until the situation became unbalanced."[23] He calls the policy of encouraging free markets "market fundamentalism" and contends that unless we find a way to regulate the natural greed in the market through a global political decision-making system, market forces will tend toward collapse, not equilibrium.

Rather than a pendulum, oscillating toward the middle, Soros likens the markets to a wrecking ball smashing everything in its path. If you didn't sell all your stocks before 2000, you can probably relate to his analogy.

Markets Are Not More Efficient Than Government
In reality, neither markets nor government are efficient. The propaganda around the desirability of free markets in part comes from problems with past government interventions in the market. Trade restrictions, wage or price controls, or attempts to curb inflation often had unintended consequences.

However, markets are easily biased as well, even with the government doing its best to rein in the giants like Microsoft. Without government oversight, the markets will always operate in favor of the big sheep that control the resources and financial flows.

In today's political climate, with all of its rhetoric around laissez-faire markets, one seldom hears of Adam Smith's belief that government "regulation in favor of the workmen is always just and equitable," though not "when in favor of the masters."[24]

In July 2002, 47 percent of people in America believed that the biggest threat to the country in the future is big government, down from a high of 65 percent in the year 2000. In that same time period, those who viewed big business as the biggest threat rose from 22 percent to 38 percent.[25] Maybe we're starting to count the right sheep.

Trade Agreements Have Not Created Free Markets
Let's say that you're a farmer in a less-developed nation. For years you grew a crop that probably did well in your climate and was in

some demand in the local economy. But with all of the trade agreements of the last thirty years, things have changed.

First, you may not be able to keep part of last year's crop for seeds anymore; the company you sell your crop to may well own a patent on that seed.

Second, while you may be following low-till or no-till practices to save topsoil, the conglomerates don't have to. "That's a tax on our cost," they say, so they fight those restrictions—and have a lower net cost of production than you do.

Third, you can only borrow from the local village bank, while your global competitors can finance this year's crop with money from anywhere in the world, at the cheapest rate available.

Fourth, now that your crop is being sold on the world market, you may find that your price is totally noncompetitive with farmers two continents away. You may have to grow what you can be competitive at, even if it's not a crop your village needs. Maybe you'll grow only vanilla or flaxseed. And if all your neighboring farmers do that, pretty soon all that will be available in the village market place are crops grown overseas, offered at global prices. And what if a crisis comes? A civil war that cuts off imports? Your village won't have food to eat.

Fifth, while you've always thought your village farm was a nice place and your family was fortunate to have a home, now your children watch television at night. "Why can't we have new clothes and potato chips and video games?" they clamor. You now see yourself as poor rather than doing fine in relation to others in the village.

And finally, the level of loans you end up with will strap you into producing the cash crops. The end result? A global pie-eating contest in which the little guy cannot compete. Instead of level markets, it's as if everyone were invited to a banquet, but the major players remove the turkey and pies from the buffet before anyone else can go through the line. And things seem only to be getting less equitable, not more. There is less and less for the lean sheep to eat.

Free Markets Aren't Free Unless Everyone Has Equal Access to Information

That every player has full information is another assumption made in most models employing market fundamentalism. Yet lack of full information *does* change behavior. This theory of "asymmetric information" earned the 2001 Nobel Prize in economics for three Americans, yet is still far from orthodox.

Think of purchasing a used car. Most people won't agree to pay the asking price because of concerns over whether the buyer is withholding information about the true condition of the car. In health care insurance, it's the seller who is wary, since the buyers hold more information about how healthy they are, forcing insurance companies to charge higher premiums for everyone.

In international markets, think of the wealth of information that our private institutional research alone, to the tune of $110 billion a year, produces in science and technology. It isn't a free market.

In financial markets, the very-real dangers of asymmetric information, insider trading, and other problems, make government regulation—intervention in the markets—necessary.

Free Markets and Macroeconomics Aren't the Only Factors in Globalization

Businesses act within communities, and those communities are living organisms, not mechanistic systems that can be predictably controlled with structural adjustment programs (SAPs). These programs are the IMF's directions for governments in developing nations to require tax hikes or service cuts so that foreign debt can be serviced.

The World Bank's programs have a failure rate of close to 70 percent in the world's poorest countries because of this lack of treating these economies as living organisms. Look at sub-Saharan Africa—there the economic problems are intertwined with problems in the education, health, and science and technology systems. Yet SAPs have resulted in shifting scarce agricultural resources into production of cash crops for export, the downsizing of civil service, and user fees for basic healthcare (which led to a 65 percent decline in the use of services in Nairobi at one clinic).[26]

Is the IMF responsible for the high level of AIDS or the lack of food production? Jeffrey Sachs, head of Columbia University's Earth Institute, puts it this way:

[I]t should take responsibility for what it is doing . . . the standard that it [used] up until now, roughly speaking, has been:

Here is what the donors are going to do, and you live within your means. And since we are against inflation, open credit creation, and instability, live within your means. . . .

We have to put the perspective a different way, which is what does the country need in order to be able to achieve some internationally-accepted goals, for example, of controlling disease, staying alive, reducing hunger, and so forth—and if that's not available financially within a macroeconomic framework as currently funded, then it is the IMF's responsibility, actually, to go back to the donors and say that's the financing gap . . . not the gap to fill some notional balance of payments. . . .[27]

Any view other than an organic one of a country's economic position leads to disasters such as attempts by the IMF to stabilize Indonesia in 1997. They provided around $23 billion to stabilize the exchange rate, but food and fuel subsidies for the poor were cut back. Riots ensued, with anger directed at business executives and their families. The unrest further discouraged foreign investments, thus countering IMF attempts at stability. The moral: Economic policies cannot be implemented as if they operate within a vacuum.[28]

Columbia Professor and Nobel Laureate Joseph E. Stiglitz developed the following view of the IMF during his stint as chief economist of the World Bank:

The IMF is pursuing not just the objectives set out in its original mandate, of enhancing global stability and ensuring that there are funds for countries facing a threat of recession to pursue expansionary policies. It is also pursuing the interests of the financial community. . . . [While it never changed its mandate,] looking at the IMF as if it were pursuing the interests of the financial community provides a way of making sense of what might otherwise seem to be contradictory and intellectually incoherent behaviors.[29]

As we've seen, the interests of the financial community revolve around the acquiring myth, which is not necessarily in the best interest of our global community.

The Actions of the Market Aren't in Everyone's Interest

On the international scene, the lean sheep aren't just people, but cultures. For example, as American companies increase overseas sales, what changes? Attitudes and habits. There is nothing neutral about advertising and marketing when it crosses cultural borders:

> [T]hose who manipulate consumer markets cannot but address behavior and attitude. That is presumably the object of the multibillion-dollar global advertising industry. Tea drinkers are improbable prospects for Coke sales. Long-lunch traditions obstruct the development of fast-food franchises and successful fast-food franchises inevitably undermine Mediterranean home-at-noon-for-dinner rituals—whether intentionally or not hardly matters. . . .[30]

The issues go deeper than our free will to consume, don't they, when one considers the marketing clout and ingenuity of corporations let loose on innocent consumers. Do we really want corporations to define cultures?

In 1991, 82.7 percent of the world's income distribution went to the 20 percent of the world's people in the wealthiest countries. Only 1.4 percent of the income went to the 20 percent in the poorest countries. That disparity has widened. Further, the bottom 20 percent, because of worldwide communications, know what they are missing. Is it any wonder they at least wonder whether Americans are greedy sheep with no concern for anyone else?

On the day that NAFTA took effect, the indigenous people of Chiapas, Mexico, initiated an armed rebellion, protesting the multinational firms that threatened their environment in the race to extract its riches.

In the year 2000, London-based Rio Tinto, one of the world's largest private mining companies, was sued by the people of New Guinea, Indonesia, and Brazil. Allegations included that the firm was responsible for environmental disasters, toxin exposure, human rights violations, and murder of residents committed in complicity with local authorities.

On September 11, 2001, the mainland of the United States was attacked by terrorists who symbolically targeted buildings that represented the country's military, government, and economic power.

These horrific acts of evil stunned us all as thousands of lives were lost and thousands more were changed forever.

Around the nation, people cried, "Why do they hate us?" As the atrocities of the Taliban surfaced, many, many people also cried, "How could we have been so blind to the plight of our neighbors for so long?" We also learned that many of the September 11 terrorists were recruited by those who saw the United States as unjust. No, the injustices don't justify their acts, but is our country just when so many people don't have enough to live on?

Perhaps the demands of the protestors in Seattle and Washington and Genoa aren't so radical. As articulated by one of the lead groups, Mobilization for Global Justice, they are quite simple, and quite in line with allowing the lean sheep to graze:

1. That the IMF and World Bank open all meetings to the public and media, just as Congress is required to do.
2. That the IMF and World Bank cancel the nearly $3 trillion in debt owed by impoverished countries that routinely spend more money servicing foreign debt than on healthcare or education. A preponderance of the debt, incidentally, arose through funding large-scale projects such as dams, oil, or mining activities— which resulted in construction contracts and resource rights for Western multinational corporations.
3. That SAPs suggested by the IMF no longer hinder people's access to food, clean water, shelter, healthcare, education, and the right to organize. For example, a hundred thousand people took to the streets in Bolivia to protest plans to privatize water distribution—a common component of these programs.
4. That the World Bank and IMF stop supporting socially and environmentally destructive projects, such as oil, mining, and gas activities, and large dams.[31]

As with many things, globalization itself isn't the problem; it's how our corporations go about it. Must it be an all-out pie-eating orgy, winners-take-all?

A BETTER FEAST THAN PIE

There is an alternative to the pie-eating contest. Think of a traditional Thanksgiving banquet. Now picture a corporation as the host of the feast, providing the turkey and stuffing and beverages. Yet instead of worrying about who gets the drumsticks, the company invites everyone they can think of. And everyone who attends brings an appetizer or rolls or sweet potatoes or cranberries to the feast.

Perhaps someone has so little that they cannot even afford to add salt or pepper to the banquet table. Instead of turning them away, the company allows them to help set the table. In some way, everyone can make a contribution.

Do you see? Instead of vying for pieces of pie—which has a finite size on our finite planet—corporations can work to add to the banquet. They aren't settling for less so much as creating a feast where everyone gets enough. They are acting as stewards of the marketplace: ensuring that the markets where they operate, produce, and sell products and services are helped, not hurt, by their operations.

The Caux Round Table, an international group of concerned business leaders, put it this way:

> Businesses established in foreign countries to develop, produce, or sell should also contribute to the social advancement of those countries by creating productive employment and helping to raise the purchasing power of their citizens. Businesses also should contribute to human rights, education, welfare, and vitalization of the countries in which they operate.[32]

The Caux Round Table was founded in 1986, recognizing that unless issues of justice were addressed, corporate actions could threaten world peace and stability. Not only is this a socially responsible stance, but setting the banquet table makes good business sense. Ask yourself the following questions:

- Is it easier to conduct business in a country with a stable government or with one that isn't supported by the people?
- Does it help commerce to have working infrastructures such as transportation, energy, communication, and finance? What if the oil companies' lobbying efforts with the

Nigerian government had supported such efforts, working with the Ogoni and other tribes?
• What about the level of education in the community? Would it help with the local infrastructures? Could a corporation begin to staff with local people?

Being a steward of the market simply makes good business sense. If we choose not to, the Bible makes clear the consequences:

> For this is what the sovereign Lord says . . . As a shepherd looks after his scattered flock when he is with them, so will I look after my sheep . . . See, I myself will judge between the fat sheep and the lean sheep. Because you shove with flank and shoulder, butting all the weak sheep with your horns until you have driven them away, I will save my flock, and they will no longer be plundered.[33]

Corporations can take steps that look socially responsible but are actually quite selfish. It is also true that being socially responsible can add to the bottom line. Few people—or businesses—can ever succeed at being totally altruistic. However, a company won't succeed at all if it doesn't consider finances as well as values.

Perhaps the business world is just beginning to learn a lesson taught long ago:

It is in giving that we receive . . .
  —St. Francis of Assisi

TOP-DOWN SOLUTIONS FOR ADDING TO THE WORLDWIDE BANQUET

From the farmers of the Great Plains to entertainers in Nashville to film editors in Los Angeles, we're part of the global pie-eating contest. Even small businesses enter the fray each time they purchase from bigger suppliers or shop for a company car or determine the nature of the product they produce. With whom will they compete? To whom will they sell? Who else is in the market?

MARKET PRINCIPLES FOR OUR CORPORATE CALLING TOWARD PRODUCTS AND PLACES

Again, a key element of stewardship of the markets is moving away from the acquiring myth toward a higher calling.

Your belief in your vision has to be bigger than your pursuit of your slice of the pie. There are plenty of needs in the world that aren't being met. Adding to the banquet means asking, "What can I bring to the table that isn't already there?"

Yvon Chouinard got the idea for Patagonia, the outdoor clothing and gear company, when he couldn't find pitons for rock climbing that wouldn't scar the rocks. He wanted useful, durable environmentally friendly products and started the company to produce them.

Robin Chase knew that Boston, Massachusetts, didn't need more cars, but public transportation wasn't always adequate for commuters from the suburbs. She developed Zipcar. For an annual fee of $75, its members have access to dozens of cars, parked at convenient locations in the metro area, on an hourly basis. The cars are perfect for short trips around town, letting commuters leave their cars at home or forego buying one altogether. (Zipcar now operates in Washington, D.C., and New York in addition to Boston).

Michael Margolis saw the explosion in need for people with knowledge of computers. He teamed up with Nick Gleason of CitySoft, a company founded to hire employees from urban neighborhoods, to form Cityskills, an alliance of eight training organizations to bridge from training to actual job placement. Margolis said, "We want to change the misperceptions that exist about who can and who can't participate in the increasingly technology-driven economy . . . this isn't about corporate charity work or a handout. The graduates coming out of these programs want to be judged by the same criteria as any other candidate."[34]

Stewards have a long-term view of what their company can add to the banquet. Instead of fighting for more pie, they are asking, "What can I bring to the table?"

The Body Shop founders Anita and George Roddick realized early on in their company's success that they could use it as a platform to do significant things in the world, as Anita attempted in her visit to the Huichol Indian tobacco farmers. The company, an international chain of skin and hair-care products, has been called a lot of things in the press, from a leader in social responsibility to morally despicable (the latter from an investigative reporter who "dug for dirt" for several years even after British courts had ruled that media allegations brought against the company were totally unfounded). Yes, their stores gain publicity when Roddick speaks at environmental gatherings or flies to meet with tribal leaders halfway around the world, but as she states,

> None of our competitors have followed our example because it doesn't create sales—believe me, if it did everyone would be doing it. . . . But what it does do is give us an identity that is recognizable. It provides motivation for our employees and sets us apart in a way that I think is more engaging and more meaningful than any advertising campaign.[35]

So what has The Body Shop done? They've refused to advertise that their products can slow the aging process; instead, they focus on healthy self-image. They've used their stores as headquarters for protest efforts and petition-signing drives. They've developed "community trade" partnerships with groups around the world, such as handmade products from Nepal (with the income going directly to a cooperative of women) and sesame seed oil from a village in Nicaragua.

And remember the eight Ogoni tribe members hung in 1995 in Nigeria? The Body Shop campaigned for their release, using company resources to help them and then, after their execution, continue efforts to release another nineteen prisoners. Those efforts met with success. For instance, the company:

- Initiated a letter-writing campaign that sent hundreds of thousands of postcards to Shell and the Nigerian government.
- Flew a group of Ogoni leaders from Nigeria to Geneva to address the United Nations Subcommission on Civil Rights.
- Offered to pay for a team of experts to assess environmental and social concerns of the Ogoni.
- Lobbied politicians and oil industry leaders.

Radical? When a consultant tried to convince Roddick that restructuring would help The Body Shop grow into a £1 billion company, she said,

> "I don't give a toss about being a bigger company. I care about becoming a better company, a more values-driven company." He didn't seem to understand what I was talking about: he didn't seem to recognize the tension I saw between growth and "losing your soul." For me, he seemed to be threatening all the things I held dear. For him, the things I held dear were an impediment to progress.[36]

Your vision should define your niche, the piece of the pie you are entitled to. In each of the above cases, the visions for the company were focused on their niches, not on their competition. They saw a need that wasn't being met and created a new company to fill that niche.

At the banquet table, you aren't in competition with the person next to you. Rather, there is plenty for all. Think back to the rain forest versus mangrove swamp image. You're looking for your rain forest niche where you can flourish indefinitely, rather than a mangrove tree that will die after rapid, consuming growth. What is the space in the market that no one else is filling?

A small, family-owned sign company was rapidly losing customers because of foreign competition. The domestic company couldn't compete due to their higher labor costs. The management team sat down to reevaluate what was unique about their company and realized that they *could* be competitive in the market for a specialized neon sign tubing they manufactured. That became their niche.

Again, the strategies aren't so much around beating the competition as around assessing what is needed in the marketplace that your firm can provide better than anyone else. For example, Amory Lovins didn't think that the major auto manufacturers were moving quickly enough to develop "green" cars. His think tank, Rocky Mountain Institute, started working on possible designs in the early 1990s. By mid-1997, thirty auto makers were in conversation with them about their Hypercar, a zero emissions vehicle with the size, safety, performance, handling, and extras of regular cars. Water is the only byproduct.

They believe the cars will be readily available in the next five to ten years.

What isn't being done or made or cleaned up or cared for that could be? That's a niche you can develop.

In each market, in each endeavor, ask, "Am I adding to the banquet or vying for pie?" Pie-eaters fight to grow fat on what is already on the table; stewards look for ways to add to the banquet so that everyone gets enough. However, simply finding a niche isn't the only criteria for determining whether you are adding to the banquet. A company also has to ask whether everyone is invited to the table—all the stakeholders, including customers and suppliers and the community as well as employees and shareholders.

Sometimes this means making investments. For example, Diageo, the company that manufactures Baileys Original Irish Cream, had always purchased the cream for the drink from the domestic milk market in Dublin, Ireland.

But by 1998, sales of Baileys reached 4.2 million cases, which required about the same amount of milk as the annual need of all of Dublin. The fragmented Irish dairy industry could not cope with this demand. Instead of looking overseas for imports, Baileys provided technical and management expertise to Irish dairy farmers to expand production and meet Baileys' needs.

Designing corporate policies to foster community goodwill makes good business sense. Clothing manufacturing firm Hannah Anderson takes a similar view of being part of a community. Its Web site celebrates the connection between community investment and corporate success:

> Giving back to the community is part of the culture at Hanna, and one that has special meaning for employees and customers alike. Giving back makes sense both socially and financially, because businesses, like people, don't live in a vacuum—companies are greatly dependent on the community! Just for starters, our workforce is educated here and our employees use the transportation system. We believe that the long-term health of our company is vitally connected to the health of our community—you can't have a healthy company in an unhealthy community.[37]

Is Hanna Anderson simply looking for PR or is social responsibility in the best interest of the company as well as the community?

One might consider the cost of not nurturing community membership—the path of the oil companies for so many decades. Exxon, for example, as it works to build a pipeline in Chad, has now hired an anthropologist to work with the local indigenous tribes. "Under pressure from activists, who have made the pipeline a focus of their campaign against globalization, Exxon has been forced to take on the unlikely role of development agency, human-rights promoter, de facto local government, and even (don't laugh) environmental watchdog."[38]

With the help of Ellen Brown, an anthropologist, Exxon has negotiated with local residents. They have built schools, funded health clinics, conducted gorilla habitat studies, paid for and participated in ritual chicken sacrifices demanded by villagers when sacred trees are felled to make room for the pipeline. Yet can an oil company whose 2001 revenues were $191.6 billion, compared with Chad's GDP of $1.4 billion, conduct itself in a way that is truly in the best interest of those villagers? Will it lead to better lives and economic development for the villagers?

The World Bank provided $93 million to Chad so it could participate as an equity partner. The Bank promised anti-globalization activists that it would cut off all loans to Chad if its government does not use the oil income for the people. They're holding 10 percent of the country's profits for future generations. Another 80 percent is supposed to go to education and heath care in a country where the current per capita annual income is $230.

There is little doubt that Exxon agreed to the terms to stay out of the protesters' spotlights. It is a step in the right direction. But will the lean sheep actually take a seat at the banquet table?

Think about your business through the eyes of Ezekiel. Place your actions on a scale to see whether justice is being done. Are there gleanings for the poor? Are public goods being devoured? Are costs counted or externalized to society or government or environment? Does everyone have enough?

Even the oil and gas industry—or perhaps because of the spotlight their misdeeds have earned, especially the oil and gas industry—is looking hard at the issues of trade:

Rich, developed countries, for example, might quit talking one way about the benefits of trade and acting another. They can dismantle protective tariffs, especially those on imports of agricultural goods. Farm tariffs starve people in some countries by enriching food producers in others. What can be right about that? Developed countries also might foreswear the use of economic sanctions as tools of foreign policy. Sanctions deliberately impoverish people and usually have no effects on the governments they're supposed to influence.[39]

The challenge is to foster the wonderful creativity the U.S. business model has unleashed without continuing the awful greed cycle.

The United States still wields the largest economic clout of any nation. That's rather like the power of the person slicing up the pie. Mom's rule still holds: The person doing the slicing should get last pick, for fairness is best judged by the receivers rather than the ones distributing the world's wealth. The acquiring myth can't overshadow the real calling of the corporation. As you look at markets, are you adding to the banquet or grabbing for pie?

How does God's love abide in anyone who has the world's goods and sees a brother or sister in need and yet refuses help? Little children, let us love, not in word or speech, but in truth and action.[40]

BOTTOM-UP STRATEGIES
FOR ADDING TO THE BANQUET

The first step is losing naïve consciousness, no longer accepting what you see as something that cannot be changed.
The second step is realizing you won't get anywhere unless you work together.
    —João Pedro Stédile, cofounder,
        Brazilian Landless Worker's Movement

Francis Moore Lappé, author of *Diet for a Small Planet,* described João Pedro Stédile as a man with "the build of a farmer and the language of a philosopher."[41] When João spoke the above words, Lappé couldn't help but note that in the United States, *naïve consciousness* is usually used to describe people who think that things *can* change. The powers of economic orthodoxy would like us to keep believing that things can't change, but perhaps the words of the apostle Paul can inspire us to work toward our corporate calling toward products and places: "Where is the wise man? Where is the scholar? Where is the philosopher of this age? Has not God made foolish the wisdom of the world?"[42]

Let's put aside the wisdom of the world and look at true philosophers like the founders of the Brazilian Landless Worker's Movement.

Twenty years ago, the Landless Worker's Movement (known as MST for its name in Portuguese) started its efforts to bring into reality the promise of the constitution adopted by Brazil in 1986 that if land wasn't serving a social function, the government had a constitutional right to redistribute it. The MST identified the most tillable idle land, organized peasant squatters to claim it, and taught them how to act as a community.

While MST's efforts have redistributed over fifteen million acres to 250 thousand families, just 1 percent of Brazil's landowners still control half the fertile land. Millions of people have no land. Free trade policies mean that large-scale agricultural firms have turned Brazil into a top-ranked exporter of sugar and coffee while millions of Brazilians struggle to find enough to eat.

The lessons of João Pedro Stédile are key, no matter where we are and no matter how much or how little influence we think we have:

- It is naïve to think that things *can't* change. Our recent collective memories of the Berlin Wall and apartheid in South Africa should prove this once and for all time.
- Working together is the only possible solution to the global problems of greed.

In the chapter on our corporate calling for products and places, we brought together two enormous themes: first, the global pie-eating contest that has brought about unconscionable disparities between the rich and the poor, and second, the need for corporations to redefine their competitive drive as a search for ways to add to the banquet. As individuals, these themes tie together in two ways. First, how do we redefine our own work in ways that add to the banquet? Second, how do we as citizens of the earth conduct ourselves so that we aren't fueling the pie-eating contest?

ADDING TO THE BANQUET

In a way, the MST sets a model for the smaller players. They didn't ask to participate in the agricultural export market, demanding their share of the pie. Instead, they simply went about reclaiming unused land to feed workers. It's a dramatic example, but small companies are finding ways to do the same thing by redefining their niche. They have to or they'll be trampled by the bigger players.

A third-generation family business had built its reputation and market share on customer intimacy—meeting the needs of each client through customized service, design innovations, and manufacturing specifications. While their products were seldom the cheapest in the marketplace, the customization added value.

However, a couple of years ago, the rules of the game changed. Their biggest customer, a Fortune 500 firm, decided to put its product specifications out on the Web to eight or nine bidders. The family business instantly saw that the competitive bidding process had driven prices below their profit margins and declined to enter the fray. The customer in essence changed the rules of the game, saying, "We want all of your value but at generic prices." One of the family firm's sales reps said, "This takes the fun out of it. Our marginal value is real; we give something above price, but now they're trying to commoditize us."

This company decided to step away from the biggest players in their customer base and redefined their niche without them.

Monitoring the Pie-Eaters

Anita Roddick told protestors in Seattle that what CEOs, corporations, and the WTO fear most is a consumer revolution. If we learned about the circumstances under which our clothing, toys, electronics, or food products are manufactured, would it change our habits? Or might we take action?

For example, think of the thousands of businesses that sell the products manufactured by Disney, Mattel, and Hasbro. In May 2002, the *Washington Post* documented systematic violations by the Chinese factories that make the toys for these companies. The violations included the following:

- Mandatory daily shifts of fifteen hours or more
- Two-month delays in wage payments
- Fines for bathroom breaks longer than five minutes
- Air temperatures above 90 degrees.

The companies denied the allegations, sending form letters attesting to their monitoring systems. However, they refused to disclose the names of the factories and would not publish their monitoring reports.

Mattel's Web site contains one monitoring report, for the factory that makes Hot Wheels and Matchbox cars, chosen because it is controlled and operated by Mattel. The report reveals illegal sixty-hour weeks, temperatures in excess of 104 degrees, and noxious fumes in this factory. Might the *Washington Post's* research have found even worse conditions at nonmonitored factories if this was the results at a monitored one?[43]

Distributors of these products can add to the banquet by working to have Disney, Mattel, and Hasbro live out their codes of conduct and monitoring. Consumer boycotts are difficult to organize, but think of the clout these companies would have to change the working conditions of thousands of Chinese if they decided it was part of their corporate calling. For example, conditions at many textile factories changed after groups of college students in the United States banded together, refusing to purchase school logo merchandise that was made under sweatshop conditions.

Appropriate Distribution

To repeat, the goal of defining a market niche is to add to the banquet rather than gobble up the pie. If you are not among the decision-makers at your workplace, there are still things to do to nudge the company toward stewardship of the markets where they do business.

Listen to other voices. The Internet is making it easier to listen to all stakeholders in a company in many ways. For example, the Ogoni tribe of Nigeria, the group that stood up to Shell Oil, has its own Web site. With the Internet, it is easy to check out a company's statements against those of other stakeholders. You can easily check out what nongovernment organizations (NGO's) and the people of other countries are saying about company operations overseas or at home.

Push for fair trade. Different from *free trade,* fair trade practices seek to return fair profits to the producers of goods as well as fair wages to workers around the world. The goal is global economic justice, and the criteria for being certified as operating under fair trade guidelines are quite specific:

- Paying a fair wage in the local context
- Offering employees opportunities for advancement
- Providing equal employment opportunities for all people
- Engaging in environmentally sustainable practices
- Being open to public accountability
- Building long-term trade relationships
- Providing healthy and safe working conditions within the local context
- Providing financial and technical assistance to producers whenever possible
- Ensuring that there is no abuse of child labor[44]

Examples include the fair trade coffee market, where coffee growers who participate receive as much as 60 percent more than the market price for their harvest. Another major area of fair trade is handcrafted goods and artwork. Normal market practices allocate only a few cents of the final purchase price to the artisan living halfway around the world from the point of sale; through fair trade enterprises, the artisan receives 15 to 30 percent of the article's market value. Teas, chocolates, and a growing list of other commodities are available through certified fair trade channels. Consider urging your company to purchase fair trade beverages or other items to support this global movement.

The fair trade movement also works toward satisfactory working conditions, that is, protection of children and improvement of sweatshop conditions. Consider checking into where company logo sportswear is manufactured or other items your office may have.

Consider your own consumer patterns. Focusing the spotlight on oil company practices changed how Exxon structured its pipeline construction project in Chad. The sweatshop boycotts have made a difference. The volume of Free Trade coffee sold in the United States doubled between 2000 and 2001. How we spend our dollars can influence the biggest corporations—if we band together.

It is true that working to add to the banquet table may increase the price we pay. However, do we want to grab for the biggest piece of pie—by paying less for our coffee or our bracelets or our tennis shoes? Or do we want to stop trampling the grass?

Debates rage over whether the emphasis on economic justice actually harms the very workers overseas that these movements are supposed to help. That is the equivalent of saying, "We *have* to keep buying things made under conditions we wouldn't tolerate. There's no alternative."

For a moment, consider the life of Li Chunmei, one of the perhaps 200 million day laborers in China's private factories, most of which are backed by foreign investors. Li Chunmei grew up in a mountain village in Sichuan Province. She finished her third-grade year in school, then joined her parents and older sister in tending the scattered wheat and rice fields that terrace the hillsides.

When Li Chunmei turned fifteen, a three-day bus ride took her to the factory district of the Pearl River Delta. Her family needed money; she didn't want her father to work so hard. There she worked as a runner in a stuffed toy factory, racing pieces between workers on an assembly line, often from 8:00 in the morning until midnight, with a ninety-minute lunch hour and thirty minutes for dinner. For this she earned at most $65 a month, less room and board charges.

But then she was transferred to a new factory. They needed more workers for the busy season. The new boss often kept the workers past two in the morning, every day for sixty days straight. Two months went by without a paycheck. When Li skipped a night shift due to exhaustion, she was docked three days' pay.

One night, after being on her feet for sixteen hours, she told her roommates that she was worn out and hungry. As she massaged her legs, she said, "I want to quit and go home."

In the middle of the night, Li Chunmei started coughing up blood. Her roommates called for an ambulance, but it arrived too late.

Her death wasn't unusual. The Chinese workers have a name for the way Li Chunmei died: guolaosi, death due to overwork. According to local journalists, dozens perish from guolaosi in the Pearl Delta Factories each year, where clothing, toys, and electronics labeled "Made in China" are made for markets around the world.[45]

Would campaigning for economic justice possibly harm workers like Li Chunmei more than they are already being harmed? Or are we going to consider our role as citizens of the world, where workers like Li Chunmei are our sisters and brothers? James Kuntsler, author of *The Geography of Nowhere*, reminds us: "The trouble with being consumers is that consumers have no duties or responsibilities or obligations to their fellow consumers. Citizens do. They have the obligation to care about their fellow citizens, and about the integrity of the town's environment and history."[46]

Changing the forces that drive our current mode of "free trade"—a system that has transferred great wealth into the hands of a few at the expense of many—involves forces of governments, businesses, greed, caste systems, and a myriad of institutions that seem immovable. But again if we're asking how, we've missed the bigger point of "We are going to say yes to making the changes."

Remember the words of João Pedro Stédile: "The first step is losing naïve consciousness, no longer accepting what you see as something that cannot be changed. The second step is realizing you won't get anywhere unless you work together."

We can say "yes" and add to the worldwide banquet, as individuals, as businesses, and as countries.

The test of our progress is not whether
we add more to the abundance
of those who have much; it is whether
we provide enough for those who have too little.
—Franklin Delano Roosevelt[47]

CHAPTER 6

PEOPLE

THEY'RE HUMAN BEINGS, NOT HUMAN RESOURCES

Life is uncertainty, surprise, hate, wonder, speculation,
love, joy, pity, pain, mystery, beauty,
and a thousand other things we can't yet imagine.
Life is not about controlling . . . life is eternal,
perpetual becoming, or it is nothing. . . .
At bottom, desire to command and control is a deadly,
destructive compulsion to rob self and others of the joys
of living. Is it any wonder that a society whose worldview,
whose internal model of reality, is based on belief
of the universe and all therein as machines
should turn destructive?[1]
—Dee Hock, founder, VISA International

A S DAVID APPROACHED THE FRONT ENTRANCE OF THE HIGH-
tech firm, he checked his watch, then took a moment to walk
around the abstract but graceful sculpture nestled among the formal flower beds that led up to the door. David was no expert, but
it looked like an original Henry Moore.

Once inside the lobby, David stopped again, captivated by the pattering cadence of the splashing fountains. The sounds echoed off the marbled walls and stairs, creating the peaceful aura of a riverside grotto.

Above the relaxing regularity of the fountains, he caught the sounds of hammers and drills. Then he noticed construction workers installing the last of the ceiling panels. Only a few of the firm's departments had moved into this opulent new headquarters building; the rest would make it their home in a few weeks—after layoffs were announced. David had been invited by the head of the human resources department to present alternatives for both outplacement counseling and for group sessions for continuing employees.

The HR director met him at the elevator and said, "We'll meet in here, but can I ask you to help me grab a couple of folding chairs? We're delaying furniture expenditures for as long as we can . . . right now I'm working off a card table instead of a desk!"

David avoided commenting on the contrast between the conference room's cherry paneling and the folding chairs as he tested his seat for stability. Just as he sat down, the CEO's right-hand man walked in, the vice president charged with determining who and how many would be let go the following week.

The HR director began, "I wanted to bring David in because I've seen the effects of layoffs before. I'm afraid that morale will tank around here if we don't hold the kinds of sessions David facilitates with the employees who stay."

"I'm more afraid that morale will tank if we don't stem this earnings skid," the vice president countered. "You know, I've run the financials on this under every scenario, and with the twenty-five hundred in layoffs I've recommended, we'll be back on track. We'll be world class again by this time next year."

David passed a description of his counseling services to the vice president and said, "Let me mention a couple of things from our experiences at other companies."

As David explained, the vice president listened patiently, but after a pause said, "I just don't think we need to do this. Our employees will understand the need for layoffs. Besides, we can't afford to do it. We'd be scrambling to purchase everything for this building even without the drop in sales."

David said, "I know you haven't budgeted it, but you can't afford *not* to do it. In fact, you'll pay for it one way or the other, through lost productivity or through services such as we offer."

The VP shrugged. "Come see us in a year. I think you'll be surprised at the spirit of our staff. They want to be on the cutting edge and they'll give us their all."

But it was the VP who was surprised as the predictions of the HR director and David came true. Instead of being world class a year later, the company was preparing for a second round of layoffs. In the third round, the VP lost his job.

The senior management of this company made the mistake of thinking that the costs and benefits of cutting the workforce could all be added up on a spreadsheet. But "soft" costs can be just as real, such as the decrease in employee loyalty or lost productivity as teams struggle to regroup without some of their members. We have a new term for the disorder that affected this vice president and thousands of people like him throughout corporate America:

> androidism [an´ droid iz em], n. fr. E. android [L. *androeides* and E. *android* an automaton with a human form]
> 1. a belief that people can function like robots. 2. a system that assumes that any human being can be substituted for any other. 3. a malady whose root cause is the belief that productivity and time on the job are in a linear relationship.

Androidism manifests itself in many ways. It exists not only in corporations, but in nonprofit organizations, churches and synagogues, schools, and even in families. If you don't recognize the following symptoms in your own firm, think of where you've heard tales from others.

No Purpose beyond a Paycheck

Androidism assumes that people are primarily motivated by paychecks. However, research by Dr. Michael Lerner, a rabbi and writer, revealed that "middle Americans often experience more stress from feeling that they are wasting their lives doing meaningless work than from feeling that they are not making enough money."[2]

At some point, we want to feel that we *counted* for something; our disillusionment fuels the high use of Prozac and the frequency of midlife crises. Yet in the theories of androidism, the purpose of work doesn't matter. It's as if a computer model were determining the value of work; meaningfulness isn't quantifiable for input into such a model.

How much better would it be if every employee had a sense of both an individual and a corporate calling? What if we realized that we are a part of something bigger than ourselves, working on purposes much bigger than anything we could accomplish on our own? A model like that was placed in front of us two thousand years ago, a model that emphasizes that there is nothing mechanical about working together and that each person plays a vital role. While the model describes the church, it applies to any business that embraces the idea of having a corporate calling: "Now you are the body of Christ, and each one of you is a part of it."[3]

No Investment in People
Proponents of androidism believe that new employees are easily programmed to do the work of those who have left.

David had lunch with an old friend who had recently taken a new sales job. The friend's first line was, "People are treated more and more like commodities these days. This company didn't give me so much as a day's training on their products and services."

The friend confided what had happened the week before. Just six months into the job, his manager put him on performance warning: "You're not making your numbers." Then the truth came out. The company routinely hires a hundred new sales reps, figuring that five or six will actually make it. Instead of investing in training, they play a numbers game.

Perhaps their game has the same net results, both in terms of successful sales reps and bottom-line impact, but it ignores the fact that sales reps are people. David's friend, despairing over how he could have failed so completely, actually checked himself into a hospital. He was so depressed that he worried he might take his own life. A person's very being is threatened in this kind of game.

To perform, people need to feel that someone is investing in their future, believing that they are capable of learning and evolving, unlike an android. Investing in training is one way this is shown. Besides, knowledge and experience have value: Hewlett-Packard estimates that it costs them $150,000 in time, lost productivity, and other costs before a single new engineer can actually do the work of an experienced one.

We are interconnected, and each of us is worth more to the whole than any balance sheet statistic shows. How much better off would businesses be if they recognized this truth: "The body is a unit, though it is made up of many parts; and though all its parts are many, they form one body"?[4]

Treatment As Interchangeable Parts

In androidism, there is nothing unique about any individual. One large department of a corporation told its two best managers, "At the end of the year one of you will be promoted to vice president over the department. The criteria will be your performance in the next twelve months."

That methodology, explicit in this case but implicit in ever so many corporations, overlooked several factors:

- The enforced competition between the two managers meant that they would be pitting their employees against each other.
- The stress of the situation would affect the judgment of both managers.
- At the end of the year, the loser would have to leave to save face, an outcome that could have been avoided if each of these talented individuals had instead been groomed for alternative positions rather than treated as interchangeable vice presidents.

That attitude betrays ignorance of a truth that each person has a unique role to play:

If the whole body were an eye, where would the sense of hearing be? If the whole body were an ear, where would the sense of smell be? But in fact God has arranged the parts in the body, every one of them, just as he wanted them to be. If they were all one part, where would the body be? As it is, there are many parts, but one body.[5]

No Recognition of Value

In a company infected with androidism, the value of employees is measured in terms of the prestige of their position. They are static, incapable of making contributions beyond that expected of someone at their level, nor are they expected to want to evolve and grow.

Unlike cogs in a machine, people aren't interchangeable or easily replaced. They carry with them a knowledge of the relationships and networks and unwritten rules and history and culture of an organization that cannot be measured or quantified. Companies actually recognize this, but because they can't measure it, their attitude comes off like this:

> You're expendable. We don't want to fire you, but we will if we have to. Competition is brutal, so we must redesign the way we work to do more with less. Sorry, that's just the way it is. And one more thing—you're invaluable. Your devotion to our customers is the salvation of this company. We're depending on you to be innovative, risk-taking, and committed to our goals. Okay?[6]

Instead, we need managers who take to heart:

> The eye cannot say to the hand, "I don't need you!" And the head cannot say to the feet, "I don't need you!" On the contrary, those parts of the body that seem to be weaker are indispensable, and the parts that we think are less honorable we treat with special honor. And the parts that are unpresentable are treated with special modesty, while our presentable parts need no special treatment.

No Acknowledgment of the Human Spirit

Androidism also assumes that outside forces don't affect a worker's productivity. No stress is created by layoffs, office politics, changes in working conditions or benefits, or the performance of other employees.

In reality, lack of trust in employees often fosters control strategies that are stressful. Karen Nussbaum, former president of 9 to 5, a clerical worker's union, reports that "Twenty-six million Americans are monitored by the machines they work on, and that number is growing. I had one woman tell me her computer would flash off and on: YOU'RE NOT WORKING AS FAST AS THE PER-SON NEXT TO YOU!"[7]

Is there anyone who wouldn't be stressed by that message? And our ability to leave that stress behind is fast disappearing. In addition to overtime, people's jobs follow them everywhere via cell phones, pagers, faxes, and e-mails. Jill Andresky, author of *White-Collar Sweatshop*, used one worker's comment on the technology to title a chapter: "They Used to Use a Ball and Chain." She likens the way our jobs spill over into our personal lives to the way an oil spill spreads over waters and beaches.

In a corporate culture formed around androidism, the employee is expected to value work more than any other aspect of life. Doubt it? Otherwise, why would a software company run a magazine ad that entices executives with the line, "How do you get feedback from fifty-two busy partners over the Fourth of July weekend?"

A recent survey showed that almost half of all Americans believe their workloads are excessive; that percentage has been rising steadily.[8] Perhaps a New York executive captured the despair of the times by saying that the best part of her day was when her commuter train went through the tunnel under the river. There, her cell phone couldn't get a signal. Those were the only moments of the day she had to herself.[9]

In short, the wants of the business take precedence over the needs of the worker. The rewards, both tangible and intangible, that come from this kind of stress seldom accrue to anyone but the owners and high-level management. The burden borne by the rest is seldom acknowledged, let alone examined. Again, androidism fails to recognize the needs of the spirit. That goes against the model we've been given: "But God has combined the members of the body and has given greater honor to the parts that lacked it, so that there should be no division in the body, but that its parts should have equal concern for each other."[10]

No Recognition of Human Limitations
While much is being made of such opportunities as job sharing and part-time work, in reality more workers are putting in longer hours than ever—especially if one adds the ever-increasing time spent commuting on the congested roadways of more and more of our cities.

Remember the predictions that accompanied the dawn of the computer era? We would have shorter workweeks and longer hours for leisure. Instead, more of us are working longer hours.

People aren't machines. If they are asked to expand their workweek from forty to forty-eight hours, their work output will not increase by 20 percent, at least not for the long haul. Eventually, efficiency falters, whether because the worker is preoccupied trying to work out children's schedules or because fatigue warps good judgment.

Profits often come in part on the backs of the workers; that is, if management only takes a short-term view. With the incessant focus on quarterly profits and a glut of mergers and layoffs, people have come to accept overwork as the way things have to be. In some management circles, the resulting strain is seen as a good thing: When older employees burn out from overwork, you can replace them with younger ones with more up-to-date technical skills, lower salary requirements, and presumably fewer health problems.

In the long term, other costs become vividly obvious. Some of the documented costs include:

- Our lack of sleep. Until Thomas Edison invented the light bulb, Americans slept on average ten hours a night. Now the average is down to seven hours with many people trying to get by on six. It doesn't work. Research shows that just one hour of lost sleep results in a 25 percent drop in productivity. But instead of admitting we need rest, we try to get by. And what happens? A 1990 study by the National Commission on Sleep Disorders calculated that in terms of productivity and accidents, the indirect costs of sleep deprivation exceed $150 billion each year in this country.
- Our compromised health. Take a look at the seven top-selling drugs in the United States: three are for hypertension, two are for angina and cholesterol, and two are for the treatment of ulcers. One estimate puts the cost of blood pressure and heart disease alone at $200 billion a year in lost workdays, medical claims, and lost compensation.[11]

Businesses need to recognize the truth that when one employee is hurting, the business suffers: "If one part suffers, every part suffers with it; if one part is honored, every part rejoices with it."[12]

In summary, androidism refuses to count the hidden or intangible costs of treating people as resources instead of as human beings. Nor does it recognize that a business is a living entity instead of a mechanistic system.

THE TRUE COST OF TREATING PEOPLE LIKE MACHINES

If we require our CEOs to focus on maximizing ROI, the workforce becomes an expense to be decreased rather than part of the company's assets. Yet employees are unique, interconnected, and essential as a part of the whole business. Businesses are also organisms made up of unique, valuable, indispensable souls. When we disregard this truth, we ignore very real, very tangible costs.

Somehow our desires for meaning and purpose, for family time and the enjoyment of the gift of life are being lost in the drive for rapid economic growth. More and more experts are saying that we can't have it all. Edward Luttwak, a former Reagan administration official who is now with the Center for International and Strategic studies, says that such a contradiction persists only because we refuse to think about it.

So-called "conservatives" make speeches lauding the unrestricted market (as the best mechanism for rapidly increasing America's wealth), while at the same time saying "we have to go back to old family values, we have to maintain communities." It's a complete non-sequiter, a complete contradiction, the two of course are completely in collision. It's the funniest after-dinner speech in America. And the fact that this is listened to without peals of laughter is a real problem.[13]

The truth is, the world has changed, but organizations haven't. The world is interconnected and in sorry need of innovation. Organizations have remained hierarchical stratifications of power and slow to change. Think about it: The traditional corporate structure, the pyramid, is modeled after a *tomb,* a place for the dead, not a place for living beings.

TOMBS VS. A BODY MADE UP OF MANY PARTS

Imagine yourself at the bottom of an actual pyramid, crushed under the weight of all of those above you. At some companies, that isn't far from reality.

Picture working at a certain metropolitan bank where, as part of a strategic planning effort, Jane interviewed all of the tellers. The first group sat tight-lipped, arms crisscrossed in a huff, and answered in tones dripping with sarcasm, "Everything's *fine*. We *love* our jobs." Jane surmised that the head teller had instructed them to say nothing, so she tried a different tack, telling a story of a great contribution made by tellers at another bank during a similar planning process.

The head teller exploded, "As if I'd be invited to the sessions. The bank has made it clear that I—that every one of us—can be replaced if we complain about anything."

"Yes," the others chorused, "they treat us as if we're a dime a dozen and can be replaced any time." A few volunteered stories of inconsiderate action by management.

Jane assured them that as the most visible part of any bank to its customers, tellers are always of value. "Not here . . ." the head teller mumbled.

Later in a debriefing meeting with the bank president, Jane conveyed the tellers' perceptions, "They feel treated as if they're only worth a dime a dozen and can be replaced."

The president growled, "They *are* a dime a dozen and they *can* be replaced. It takes no skill whatsoever to be a teller."

The result of the president's attitude? High teller turnover and a customer survey that complained that they seldom saw familiar faces at the bank; the place was unfriendly, more like a mausoleum than a thriving financial center for a community.

Now picture yourself as an employee of a high-tech manufacturing firm in the same town. Reell Precision Manufacturing suffered a $200,000 loss when its core business of springs and hinges for laptop computers fell off sharply in 2001.

Co-CEOs Bob Carlson and Steve Wikstrom talked to their employees about the dilemma—and managers and workers alike elected to take wage cuts rather than lay anyone off. They exempted those at the bottom of the pay structure from the cuts.

What happened next Carlson attributes to "a motivated sales staff and designers and workers who own a piece of the company and were ready to make the most of a business pickup."[14] Revenues increased more than 25 percent in 2002. Despite the seemingly fragile recovery, management paid out full bonuses and restored the wage cuts early in the year, as soon as the sales figures showed the increase. Wikstrom says, "We are deeply convinced that people are most likely to behave ethically when the motivation for such behavior comes from within. Our efforts focus primarily on providing an environment, policy benefit and relationships that inspire rather than coerce ethical behavior."[15]

In other words, management policies are fostering relationships and personal growth. Employees are treated like living human beings who are vital to Reell.

Which kind of organization do you want to belong to? One where employees are interchangeable parts or where every individual is valued? One with hierarchies and power struggles or one where the contributions of every part are acknowledged? One where each person is trying to scramble to the top or where people recognize that their success depends on the success of everyone else? One where you are criticized for what you can't do or one where you are celebrated for what you *can* do?

Those are the differences between a mechanistic corporation and a living entity.

A CORPORATE MODEL FOR LIVING BEINGS

Fortunately, the image of a corporation as a living entity is beginning to gain ground in the think tanks of the world of business. Peter Senge, through his *Fifth Discipline* materials, emphasizes that corporations must move away from mechanistic models toward entities that can learn and evolve. *The Individualized Corporation* (Sumantra Ghoshal and Christopher Bartlett) discusses how we can inspire employees and build on a fundamental faith in individuals. In *Stewardship*, Peter Block emphasizes that choices should be maximized for those closest to the work. Instead of measuring behavior and style, companies should measure business results and real outcomes. Managers become coaches instead of monitors. And in *The Living Company*, Arie de Gues points out the dysfunctional nature of the mechanistic model:

On one hand, all the experts, academics, and managerial success measurements line up on the side of the economic definition. They suggest that the company's heart, the core of its nature, is the economic activity it pursues to stay alive. On the other hand is the evidence of managers' own eyes, ears, and feelings: that the core of their company's nature, its heart, is its existence as a continuous work community—in short, as a living, learning company.[16]

Instead of a pyramid, or a mechanistic model, think of a corporation as a living organism, a fruit tree if you will. Gordon MacKenzie, former Creative Paradox at Hallmark (that was the official job title he created for himself!) points out that in this model, management and corporate resources are the roots from which energy flows to the creators. Customer service contacts live amidst the branches where they can get the sunshine and air they need to be creative, instead of being weighted down at the bottom of a pyramid.[17]

If the company is a tree instead of a machine, then management tasks and the basis for decisions change radically. Let's take a look at a few key areas.

Employees. As we've seen, in the mechanistic model employees are often viewed as interchangeable parts in the system.

In the fruit tree model, hiring new employees is the equivalent of grafting new branches. Grafting is careful work, requiring the monitoring of how everything around the new branch is affected. And not just any branch can be grafted on. The new has to be compatible with the tree.

In *Good to Great* by Jim Collins, the care to be taken with hiring new employees is described as getting the right people on the bus:

> But if people are on the bus because of who else is on the bus, then it's much easier to change direction . . . the problem of how to motivate and manage people largely goes away. The right people don't need to be tightly managed or fired up; they will be self-motivated by the inner drive to produce the best results and to be part of creating something really great.[18]

Grafting new branches also implies permanence. Branches can only be taken on and off so many times. And, given how much of our lives are given to work, isn't that a good model? Find people you want to work with, who believe in what you are doing, and keep them around for the long haul.

Training. In a mechanistic model, training is an expense. Employees may be left on their own to develop the skills they need.

In caring for a living organism, training helps seedlings become all they can be. Trees are given water and fertilizer; ropes and stakes might be used gently to help them grow straight and tall; and care is taken to give them room to grow. And before any of the tending begins, gardeners place trees in the right place, with the right kind of soil and right amount of sunshine.

Our *LifeKeys* program is designed to help individuals find that right place; our *BusinesKeys*[19] process can be used for groups of employees. It helps teams value the different parts of the body—the coworker who seems more like an appendix than a right arm gets transported to a place that fits.

The process takes time as people work through identifying five aspects of who they are:

- **Life gifts** or talents, adding a deeper understanding of the theory behind the Strong Interest Inventory.
- **Spiritual gifts** through a self-discovery process that includes biblical and modern-day stories of the gifts in use (this lens is adjusted for secular settings).
- **Personality type** by exploring the theories behind the Myers-Briggs Type Indicator to identify places or atmospheres where different people might prefer to work, live, or volunteer.
- **Values** and **Passions** to discover how they might best add meaning and purpose to their lives.

For people who never realized that these elements fit together in a unique way for each human being, it may take up to nine months to discover what they are called to do. We've found, though, that the process can't be rushed by *telling* people or by having them fill out blind inventories that match them to certain jobs. For people to embrace who they are, they need to discover it for themselves and then be nurtured into believing that it is a wonderful, God-given way to be.

One person who made these discoveries long before *LifeKeys* was Fred Rogers. At a start-up public television station back in the 1950s, he was allowed to experiment with different gifts. In an interview a few months before he died, Mr. Rogers put it this way:

> Every part of who you are comes out in every assignment you have. But when I was ordained in the church, the ordination read like this: "You are to continue your work for families and children through the mass media . . ." I loved drama and music and puppetry and I liked television and I liked philosophy and religion. But the moment I realized that all of those could be used in the service of children and their families, that's when I knew who I was.[20]

What would your company be like if all of your employees knew who they were?

Mergers. In the mechanistic model, a merger simply means adding more machines to the production floor. In the merger craze of the past years, deals were justified by spreadsheets that calculated how cutting the total combined workforce by a certain percentage would provide a corresponding reduction in expenses.

It didn't work that way. It is estimated that 61 percent of mergers that took place in the last half of the 1990s destroyed shareholder wealth. While part of the problem stemmed from the inflated prices paid by buyers, one of the biggest factors was the unanticipated levels of stress and unproductive time spent trying to meld two different cultures.[21] In the fruit tree, a merger would be the equivalent of grafting together the trunks of two trees—re-creating the heart of a company.

Think of how differently mergers would be approached if viewed as a heart transplant. Instead of the acquiring company simply adding products or markets or services, dealmakers would investigate the nature of the cultures, the impact on the employees, the intangibles that can't be calculated on a spreadsheet. This is the kind of care that David and the director of the human resources department were recommending in the story that opened this chapter.

Reengineering. In a mechanistic organization, reengineering involves taking the "motor" of a company apart and putting it back after redesigning it for more efficiency. There is no sense of the impact that downsizing might have on those left behind.

In a tree, reengineering would be pruning—a necessary task, but care must be taken as to the process used as well as the timing of the procedure. The tree has to be dormant at the time its branches are cut. If pruning is done at the wrong time, it can actually kill the tree. Further, work remains to be done after the pruning; the wounded places must be covered and cared for.

Productivity. In a mechanistic organization, productivity can be improved by tuning the engines, running them for longer hours, and increasing power to the system.

For a fruit tree, that recipe spells disaster. Adding too much fertilizer or water may produce foliage in the short term, but excess leaf growth can lessen the energy for fruit production. Excess water can damage the root system.

The same is true for people. Extra energy will increase production only in the short term. Eventually people burn out. The kind of rapid growth that is praised in productivity has no equivalent in living organisms, where fast-growing cells are usually cancerous.

For example, many businesses are relying on overtime put in by a few employees rather than hiring more workers. If overtime stays in the 10 to 12 percent range of total time worked, employees benefit by receiving extra pay and employers gain flexibility by limiting the number of workers on the permanent payroll. However, a study by Circadian Technologies, Inc.,[22] details the effects of abnormal shifts and overtime hours on morale and overall productivity. When workers put in sixty or more hours per week for long periods, productivity falls by as much as 25 percent. There are no real savings. Concrete information like this study can influence corporate policies about the true costs of andriodism.

As an illustration of our obsession with productivity, look at the average annual days off (including federal holidays) around the world:

Italy	42	South Korea	26
Brazil	40	Canada	24
France	36	Japan	23
Germany	35	United States	20
Britain	30		

Do we care so little about life balance that we want to remain in last place? In Malta, businesses close at one o'clock all summer long, yet *everything gets done*. People relax, head to the island's eighty-seven beaches, enjoy the season's festivals, and read the books they don't have time for in the winter.

In the United States, in contrast, weekend getaways (complete with laptops and pagers) are fast replacing the two-week road trips that figure largely in many of our childhood memories. We need to return to a business model that allows for periods that are the human equivalent of dormancy, of recharging for the next season of growth and harvest.

Time frame. In a mechanistic organization, the outlook is short term. Managers concentrate on producing more in the current quarter. The focus on the bottom line often prevents looking toward the future. Investing in research or equipment can seem counterproductive.

In an orchard, though, the horizon is long-term. Seedlings won't produce fruit for several years, at least not enough to justify the time and effort put into ensuring that they grow properly.

The short-term horizon influences whether things such as research, training, and benefits which encourage employee wellness are seen as costs to the bottom line or investments in the future of the company. A long-term view is essential if companies are to reach toward their corporate calling.

Timing. A mechanistic organization changes according to business models. Mergers, layoffs, new incentive plans, promotions, and so forth, are done quarterly or at the urgings of the market.

In an orchard, changes are made when the timing is right. It's easier to uproot and replant trees in the fall or spring. The harvesting takes place when the fruit is ready, not when the plan says it should be done.

Value. A mechanistic corporation considers its plant, machinery, and inventory as its assets. A fruit tree knows that the whole is worth more than the sum of the parts. Separate from the trunk, what value are the leaves? And the trunk and branches are only good for firewood without the nourishment provided through roots. The fruit at first glance might seem most valuable, but it can't grow without being connected to the rest of the organism.

An organic organization recognizes the interconnectedness of all its parts and includes in its assets its social capital, defined as "the stock of active connections among people: the trust, mutual understanding, and shared values and behaviors that bind the members of human networks and communities and make cooperative action possible."[23]

A manager in an organic organization knows that the future depends not just on production or customer service efficiencies but on developing the people side of the business. Time spent on nurturing relationships and informal conversation is not wasted time. Take the case of a TV production unit that experienced productivity problems after moving to a new "purpose-built" workplace:

> It was some time before [company leaders] worked out what the problem was. It turned out that, when the architects were designing the new building, they decided that the coffee room where everyone ate their sandwiches at lunchtime was an unnecessary luxury and so dispensed with it. The logic seemed to be that if people were encouraged to eat their sandwiches at their desks, then they were more likely to get on with their work and less likely to idle time away.[24]

An organic organization, not looking to quantify the productivity of each square foot of its facilities, might more quickly recognize the social capital maxim that all business people understand instinctively: The most useful part of the workday—or a day-long meeting—is the coffee break. That's where the real work gets done.

MANAGING PEOPLE IN AN ORGANIC ORGANIZATION

Some of the key differences between the two organizational models follow. However, perhaps the most important consideration to keep in mind is that in our rapidly changing, evolving, unpredictable, chaotic world, the mechanistic model has no basis in reality. The results of continuing to model organizations after machines are systemic failures of our economic, religious, educational, governmental, and social structures. We need to change our entire way of thinking about employees so that our organizations honor them as living beings instead of treating them like androids. The contrast in style is seen in following table:

	Mechanistic Organizations	Organic Organizations
Core of management practices	Control	Trust with accountability
Goal	Compliance	Self-discipline
Manager-employee relationship	Contractual	Supportive
Rewards given for	Conformity, across-the board initiatives	Outlying opinions, innovation
Nature of corporate vision	Top-down, related to growth	Vision of corporate calling; employees develop own intentions and values around it
Measure of success	Quantitative measures	Qualitative and quantitative measures
Basis of power	Fear, employees doing what you want when you want	Emotional intelligence

Scrooge, that tight-fisted, grasping, covetous boss, models a mechanistic management style at the beginning of *A Christmas Carol*:

> The door of Scrooge's counting-house was open that he might keep his eye upon his clerk who, in a dismal little cell beyond, a sort of tank, was copying letters. Scrooge had a very small fire, but the clerk's fire was so very much smaller that it looked like one coal. But he couldn't replenish it, for Scrooge kept the coal-box in his own room; and so surely as the clerk came in with the

shovel, the master predicted that it would be necessary for them to part. Wherefore the clerk put on his white comforter, and tried to warm himself at the candle; in which effort, not being a man of strong imagination, he failed.

Imagine putting your hands into a bucket of ice water, then trying to write with a quill pen—efficiency would be drowned in the struggle to keep the quill from shaking as you shivered. Scrooge didn't understand that things you can't measure are often far more costly than the items you can account for in your budget.

In the last chapter of *A Christmas Carol*, Scrooge models for us what an "orchard" manager looks like. All of a sudden, Bob Cratchitt was a whole person to Scrooge, with a family, with needs like staying warm, with ideas and added value. Scrooge, in effect, turned his counting house into a living entity, an organic organization. In doing so, he sacrificed some of his gold in helping Cratchitt's family, but he also lost the isolation, crippling greed, and lack of purpose that had poisoned his soul for so long.

Are you part of an orchard or part of a tomb?

Scrooge was better than his word. . . . He became as good a friend, as good a master, and as good a man, as the good old city knew, or any other good old city, town, or borough, in the good old world.
—Charles Dickens, *A Christmas Carol*

TOP-DOWN SOLUTIONS FOR CORPORATE CALLING TOWARD HUMAN BEINGS

There is no single model for living companies (although the pyramid may be the least helpful). If your vision and purpose are at the heart of things, then the question becomes, "What kind of organization will help us fulfill our purpose?" Notice that we didn't say organizational structure; living systems are often fluid with cohesiveness coming through general principles rather than rigid structures.

As Dee Hock and his team set out to design a new organization, he asked, "If anything imaginable was possible, if there were no constraints whatsoever, what would be the nature of an ideal organization to create the world's premier system for the exchange of value?"[25] We know their answer as VISA—a trillion-dollar company that is owned by its members who must both compete and cooperate. Fewer than five hundred employees were necessary for its explosive growth. Its shape rose out of a few principles that emerged in trying to reach toward its purpose. In effect, VISA self-organized. There was no top-down master plan, but instead an evolving vision that turned the principles into an entity. Hock calls it a "chaordic" organism, a self-governing organization that evolved on the fringe of chaos and order.

There are some general principles that help in creating a living company. Some of these include the following.

FLATTEN THE STRUCTURE

Instead of "command and control," use trust and collaboration, increasing both the freedom and responsibility of each employee.

For example, some managers spend an inordinate amount of time monitoring the productivity of workers. Were they in their places by 8 AM? Did they stretch their lunch break? Are they typing fast enough? Are they talking to coworkers instead of concentrating on work?

Change the paradigm. Put workers in control of the work and let them schedule the time—and let the most efficient leave early if they're done. Otherwise, an elaborate cat-and-mouse game emerges, where workers aim to accomplish "just enough" during their scheduled shifts while managers watch and warn and waste their own time on monitoring activities that add nothing to the company's creativity or to the goods and services produced.

Your business may involve totally different operations, but the principle remains the same: How can the work be structured so that people take responsibility for themselves? Through rewards for productivity? Through giving them a voice in matters that pertain to them? Through letting them leave when they're "done"?

COMMUNICATE PURPOSE RATHER
THAN GOALS

Think back to the Jim Henson Company and other firms whose missions give employees a purpose beyond the paycheck. Part of a corporate calling is helping employees discover their assignments that tie into those bigger missions and believe, "You are more than your job."

In addition, while living companies can't guarantee lifetime employment, they can help their workers plan for education and work experiences that will keep them employable. This is key in a world where college graduates often find their knowledge base outdated within a few years of graduation.

In running a living company, another key element is remembering that in nature there is no such thing as a weed. It's just a plant in the wrong place. You will have employees whose assignments don't mesh with your corporate purpose. Helping them identify their own bigger purpose is more of a favor than never firing anyone.

INVOLVE THOSE DOING THE CORE WORK
OF THE ORGANIZATION IN DECISIONS

Customer contact personnel often spot trends ahead of the market. Assembly workers know what is and isn't working. Yet too often, management doesn't believe that such input—circumstantial and unsubstantiated—can be of value.

Jane's favorite "Employees Know Best" story comes from a small bank. To fulfill the bank's mission of being the friendliest bank in town, tellers greeted each customer as they came in the door. However, the teller station counters were so high that the tellers had to stand all day to see customers as they entered. The requirement to stand for eight hours was actually affecting the health of the tellers; they had joint and circulation problems.

Management said, "That's the way it has to be. They need to greet customers and we can't invest thousands of dollars in redesigning the teller stations."

We said, "Why don't you let the tellers suggest some solutions?"

Management said, "If there were a solution, we would have come up with it."

We told the tellers to meet.

A week later, the tellers said, "We've gotten two bids. It will cost $350 to have a carpenter remove the marble tops to our stations, cut away eight inches of the wood, and put the tops back on. With the tops that much lower, we'll be able to sit on stools and still see customers."

Management, after pulling feet out of mouths, said, "Here's the $350 check."

HIRE WITH CARE

After September 11, layoffs proliferated in many industries. However, Southwest Airlines retained its staff. So did the Kiplinger publishing organization. The president, Knight Kiplinger, said, "[We're] having the same really tough year as the big publicly-traded media conglomerates, but unlike most of them, we're not handing out pink slips. Our employees will weather storms together."[26] He suggested cutting executive bonuses, corporate entertaining, or even hours worked for all employees before anyone is laid off—a pattern their private business has always followed.

One of David's friends has never laid off an employee. When asked how he managed to stick to this principle in spite of layoffs at his competitors, he said, "That's easy to explain. When the company down the street hired a hundred workers, I only hired ten. I kept my workforce in line with what we were becoming."

ALLOW THE WHOLE PERSON TO COME TO WORK

Dee Hock claims that one needs four-dimensional models to describe chaordic organizations—and that fourth dimension is the spiritual and ethical.[27] To find meaning and purpose, people cannot isolate their work lives from the rest of their existence.

SAS Institute, a software company that has experienced double-digit growth for two decades, insists that employees seek balanced lives, encouraging a thirty-five-hour workweek. The switchboard is turned off at 5 PM and the main gate is shut an hour later. David Russo, their vice president for human resources, admits that a few years ago their rivals considered them insane, but "in the last two years, we've had twenty companies—some really big companies—come down and study what we're doing."[28] They attribute their 98 percent customer retention rate to low employee turnover (and they estimate that lack of turnover saves them about $70 million a year, which certainly covers any increased staffing needs that result from shorter workweeks).

Husky Injection Molding Systems Ltd., a Canadian firm, placed second in an annual Canadian ranking of the most socially responsible firms. The founder, Robert Shad, works to ensure that company policies reflect his personal philosophies. They adhere to environmental health and safety practices. The wellness programs for employees include an on-site gym, a cafeteria that features health foods, and incentives for employees to bike to work. Community service is rewarded and a twenty-four-hour daycare center, professionally staffed, provides peace of mind for working parents.

Shad's philosophies have resulted in substantial lowering of waste-disposal costs, lower health insurance premiums, improved morale, and reduced absenteeism, but the millions in savings aren't the real goal. He says that you have to believe in the programs. They can't be expendable when times are difficult. Things like daycare are sacred in his vision of the workplace.[29]

NURTURE CREATIVITY INSTEAD OF DELIVERING CONTROL

In his book *Stewardship,* Peter Block suggests that true empowerment allows employees to be creators of the organization to which they belong. They define their own purposes and make a commitment, an emotional investment in their tasks.[30]

Often the term *empowerment* is used to justify increased workloads while retaining actual control of what employees do and aspire to, but here it means letting the employees share in the vision of what they might become.

Jane once worked with a group of bank presidents who weren't used to being empowered. After the first day of a strategic planning workshop for these affiliated banks, the presidents were asked to spend the evening brainstorming the opportunities they saw in their markets. Instead, they literally headed to the bars. The quality of their input to the process indicated that they didn't think what they had to say mattered.

The owner chose to give them a quiz the next day. What had he said was the vision of the organization? Face after face turned red as the presidents acknowledged that they had no idea.

The owner said, "It's simple. You're to be better. Better than before at serving customers, better than the bank across the street in ways that only you can discover. That's it. Figure out how to do it."

In effect the owner was saying, "It's up to you to define 'better.' I'm not handing you a plan." He handed them the responsibility and the room exploded in an outpouring of creativity as the presidents started to imagine their futures.

BUILD ON STRENGTHS, NOT WEAKNESSES

For decades, employee reviews emphasized identifying a person's weaknesses and then setting goals to overcome those weaknesses. While there will always be skills that each of us needs to develop, there's another way to accomplish the task: building on strengths.

What if reviews consisted of helping employees envision what they might become? What if responsibilities were given to helping develop those strengths?

The Container Store, retailers of storage and organizational products, ranked second in *Fortune's* list of the best companies to work for. Each new full-time sales representative receives an average of 245 hours of training; the average for all of their employees is over 160 hours of training every year. The company says they focus on matching "employees' strengths with the needs of the company, focusing on talent rather than titles. . . . Extensive training programs, customized to the individual and job function. . . ."[31] Employees looking to build a career with The Container Store attend a three-day continuing education class as an introduction to possibilities within each department. This gives them a chance to explore different areas within the company that they wouldn't normally be in contact with.

One of the results of this investment in employees is a voluntary turnover rate of only 8 percent, compared to the retail sector average of 48 percent.[32] Helping employees discover where their talents fit into the corporate calling pays off.

CREATE EMOTIONAL INTELLIGENCE, SOCIAL CAPITAL

As you work to make changes, the first step is to recognize the social capital you already have. Sometimes it makes sense to reform teams around products or services rather than having separate departments for legal, financial, and other functions. However, some times those departments are functioning so cohesively as teams, sharing knowledge and experience, that the losses will outweigh the gains from creating cross-functional teams.

The second step is to help everyone recognize the level of social capital others see in them. Gandhi once said, "Power is granted from those below." There are safe, anonymous, 360-degree feedback processes that allow for this. For example, a president of a small manufacturing firm believed that it was his responsibility to suggest solutions for every problem. Frequently, he locked himself in his office until he had time to think through different alternatives. When he presented his ideas in staff meetings, he grew frustrated that no one offered thoughtful critiques. Feedback helped the president understand that his top employees felt cut out of the process. His solutions always seemed final when they heard about them. The president developed a new process that gathered their ideas early on—and found that his management team became more involved and more supportive.

The third step is valuing people for more than their technical and leadership skills. Who are the counselors and sages and cheerleaders and coaches in your midst? The emotional intelligence displayed by them may be more important than any technical skill.

SHIFT RESPONSIBILITY TO EACH EMPLOYEE TO CARRY OUT THEIR CORPORATE CALLINGS

If you are treating your employees as living, whole human beings, then their responsibility becomes completing their assignments to the best of their abilities. Create the vision, help each person see how their individual life-long assignment fits within that vision, and impress upon them that fulfilling it is their calling. No level of financial reward can be substituted for the motivation one gets from feeling called to do something.

It's broad, it's a long way from where we are, but you can keep your sights on evolving into a living company by continually asking a few key questions:

- Am I honoring differences of opinion and outlandish ideas?
- Am I running a four-dimensional company, where spirituality and ethics are welcomed?
- Are the rules fair to executives and entry-level employees alike?
- Are we pursuing a purpose bigger than profits?

If you can answer "yes" to every question, you are evolving toward a living, dynamic, entity that values human beings.

BOTTOM-UP STRATEGIES FOR OUR CORPORATE CALLING TOWARD HUMAN BEINGS

In our time, we workers are being called to reexamine
our work: how we do it; whom it is helping or hurting;
what it is we do; and what we might be doing
if we were to let go of our present work and follow a deeper call.
—Matthew Fox[33]

Jane once worked with a team of production managers who had a wonderful problem: they needed to double their usual output to fulfill a huge order from a new customer. To enrich their thinking about the situation, Jane introduced a problem-solving strategy to consider multiple viewpoints.

First, the facts: "We're on schedule so far." "We can handle the workload by running a third shift." "Even the president is taking his turn at the third shift, on the machine floor." "Even with the overtime wages, the profit margin is extremely high." "The officers aren't taking extra pay."

Then, the possibilities: "With the increased revenue, we'll be able to do some long-needed technology upgrades." "If we keep this new customer long-term, we'll have an incredibly solid revenue base."

The pros and cons: "We're vulnerable to a machine breakdown and need a contingency plan." "We need to make sure we aren't ignoring other customers."

Finally, we got to the impact on people: "Morale is good, especially when the president takes his shift." "People are excited that this customer might mean financial security." The conversation continued in gleeful optimism until one man stood up and said, "We're forgetting that all of us are *people*. How long do you think we can rotate that third shift before our health, our families, or our relationships break down?"

The room went silent for at least a full minute. Then the conversation turned to generating a whole new set of possibilities to meet the new demand levels while phasing out the horrendous overtime burden. That one lone voice changed everyone's perspective.

One person, or a small group of people working together, can make a tremendous difference when it comes to how people are treated in a team or a department. Demonstrate the positive impact on productivity to the rest of the company and you can perhaps change the world.

However, the mechanistic model is deeply imbedded in the management and organizational behavior literature that permeates business schools. Here are a few strategies you can use to argue the other side of the issue, champion the idea of a living company, and challenge the powers-that-be to put people first.

FILL IN THE MISSING QUESTIONS

Take to heart the words of the apostle Paul: "The eye cannot say to the hand, 'I don't need you!' And the head cannot say to the feet, 'I don't need you!' On the contrary, those parts of the body that seem to be weaker are indispensable, and the parts that we think are less honorable we treat with special honor."[34]

Companies need the input of every employee, for each part of the living company has a unique viewpoint. Poor—and costly—decisions often result when "heads" or "mouths" or "arms" make key decisions without listening to the "ankles" or "toes" of the workforce.

One of the ways to ensure that all voices are being heard is to identify the main voices that are listened to. What is the prevailing mindset of the corporation? The breakthrough Jane facilitated with the production management team came about through the constructs of personality type, the theory behind the Myers-Briggs Type Indicator tool. This theory holds that people have *preferences* for how they take in information and make decisions. When we are aware of our preferences, however, we can act to compensate for them.

For example, the dichotomy of Thinking and Feeling describes how we prefer to make decisions. Those with a Thinking (T) preference prefer to rely on objectivity/logic, cause/effect or other systematic models for making decisions. These methods are wonderful for bringing consistency and clear reasoning to the process.

Those with a preference for Feeling (F) make decisions by subjectively placing themselves into a situation and considering how everyone will be affected. The production manager who said "How long do you think we can rotate that third shift before our health, our families, or our relationships break down?" approached his decisions from the Feeling side.

Studies consistently show that 80 percent or more of the business executives in the United States have Thinking preferences, compared with closer to 50 percent of the general population. To see whether Thinking decision-making dominates your place of work, recall the dialogue or communication around a decision. Which kinds of issues were given the most weight?

Thinking	Feeling
• Pros and cons of alternatives	• Impact on individuals
• Objectivity, consistency	• Consensus, harmony
• Costs/cost savings	• Needs, viewpoints of all stakeholders
• Predicted outcomes	• Values to be honored
• Consequences of acting/ not acting	• Intangible losses from acting/ not acting

Truly excellent decisions come when questions generated from both sides of the chart are given equal weight in the process. Therefore it is appropriate to push back when a discussion is dominated by Thinking types. Examples might include the following:

Thinking: "By cutting ten employees, we'll realize a savings equal to their salaries plus benefits."

Feeling: "But what about the lost productivity because of the disruption to the employees they work with? Downtime because they wonder if they, too, might be cut? A decrease in loyalty because employees may need to look out for themselves?"

Thinking: "Let Smith quit. We can replace him."

Feeling: "But Smith is the one who keeps everyone smiling. At times, he's been instrumental in keeping the team working together. We can replace his technical skills, but not his ability to turn conflict into productivity."

Think ahead, using the Feeling paradigm, and prepare to be a balance to the Thinking worldview.

MODEL THE WORLD YOU WANT TO SEE

You've heard it before, but taking a stand on what you believe can truly bring about change. Jane used to work with a man named Mike, who insisted on leaving the office on time nearly every day. He quipped, "I work 'second shift' at home and can't be late." His wife took evening college classes and Mike needed to be there for his preschool-age boys. Mike knew his job and everyone else's as well. He pitched in to get everyone out the door on time.

However, the rest of the department was quickly developing a martyr mentality, "Ooooh, we have so much to do. I didn't get out of here until 7:00." "I ate breakfast, lunch, and dinner at my desk." "I didn't even see my kids yesterday . . ."

One Friday afternoon, Mike's boss dropped off a note requesting major changes to a project—by Monday morning. Amidst our cries of, "He did that just to make us work the weekend," Mike said, "We aren't going to. And it's my call. I'll set up a computer program to do the job first thing Monday, the changes will be letter-perfect by Tuesday, and if there's a problem I'll take the blame."

And on Tuesday, when our boss tried to accuse us of insurrection, Mike calmly stood his ground. No one needed to work the weekend. Everything was ready.

The incident changed management's attitude. Yes, we stayed late occasionally when the need was great, but martyrdom was replaced by a team effort to balance work and family.

It can happen, especially with the efforts of someone like Mike who backed up his beliefs with the skills to efficiently do the work.

What are the issues with people in your department? If lower-level people aren't treated with respect, how could you model change? If coffee breaks or lunching together are seen as inefficient, can you be vocal about the problems solved and important issues raised at these times when employees gather? If qualities such as being able to nurture and support others aren't valued, how can you tout their worth? In *The Soul of a New Machine* by Tracy Kidder,[35] such people are called "health-engendering people." And often, they're the unaccounted-for cornerstone of success in teams.

USE DOLLARS AND CENTS (AND MINUTES AND HOURS)

Because objective evidence speaks so well to those who cling to mechanistic models of the world of work, speaking their language can be more successful in bringing change than talking in terms of "life balance" or "treating employees as individuals."

Figure out the cost of training new "expendable" employees. Every kind of labor is skilled labor. If you doubt that, imagine yourself for a moment as a waiter in a busy café. Get the right orders to seven tables in fifteen minutes or less. Remember what everyone wants. Make the salads, pour the beverages, stop by with refills before the coffee gets cold. Smile all the time and have a few witty things to say. Nurture relationships with the chefs so that your customers get the choicest cuts while they're still hot. Mark any changes to the customer's initial orders. Keep crackers in your pocket (and crayons) for hungry, tired children. Memorize the specials. . . . There's a similar list for every job.

There are lots of other things to quantify. How about the number of employees who come down with colds or the flu after (or during) a stressful period of overwork? Or the extra dollars spent on a dumb decision by management because they didn't ask employees what they really needed. Or the loss of the underappreciated worker who quit.

Remember, in the mechanistic model, employees are seen as an expense, not an asset. All of us need to emphasize in everything we do that:

- People aren't machines and cannot be treated as such over the long haul.
- There are things that people do better than machines—and things that machines can't do at all.

Kirk: *I know Bob Wesley, I knew he wouldn't attack [the Enterprise] without making absolutely sure there was no other way. His "logical" selection was compassion. It was humility, Mr. Spock.*

McCoy: *They are two qualities no machine ever had. Maybe they are the two things that keep men ahead of machines. Care to debate that, Spock?*

Spock: *No, Doctor. I merely maintain that machines are more efficient than human beings. Not better . . . they are not gods.*[36]
—Star Trek, The Ultimate Computer

CHAPTER 7

OUR PLANET

TENDING THE ORCHARD
WHILE TAPPING THE TREES

It is said that to everything, there is a season.
The world today needs to usher in a season
of transformation, a season of stewardship.
Let it be a season in which we make a long overdue
investment in the survival and security of future generations.[1]
—Kofi Annan, U.N. Secretary-General

WHEN JANE'S CHILDREN WERE PRESCHOOLERS, ONE SUMMER she decided to "hatch" a monarch butterfly. On her morning walk, she inspected a roadside patch of milkweed plants. Sure enough, a yellow, green, and black-striped caterpillar clung to one of the leaves. She plucked the leaf it was currently nibbling, along with several more for its dinner and breakfast.

Once home, she and the children cut a hole in the top of an ice-cream bucket, lined it with paper towel, added a sturdy twig or two and gently placed the caterpillar and its food inside. By that night, the pudgy creature had already hung itself upside down on the twig, its cocoon partially formed.

Each morning for a couple of weeks, the children carefully checked for any change in the cocoon's appearance. Finally, one morning, it seemed translucent; the bright orange and black of the monarch could be seen. They took the bucket outside and watched as the cocoon pulsed and split open, the delicate wings unfolding to dry in the sunshine. Within minutes the butterfly took flight, encircling the children, then flying off toward the park behind their home.

Jane hasn't found a single monarch caterpillar since.

The milkweed patch was replanted with grass; the few plants she's found elsewhere in her suburb show no signs of being nibbled. And she's only seen a handful of the butterflies each summer.

Debate rages over whether monarch butterflies are actually endangered, as do debates over most environmental issues. However, nearly 50 percent of the forests in Mexico where monarchs overwinter have been logged; what thirty years ago was nearly continuous high-quality forest is now a series of islands of trees for the millions of butterflies that migrate there annually. Without the forest's lush canopy for protection, a winter storm in 2002 killed up to 80 percent of the colonies.

Further, in the United States, heavy use of herbicides on corn and soybean fields has decreased milkweed plants, the only food monarch caterpillars eat.

If you've been numbed by environmental Chicken Little's crying too frequently that "The sky is falling!" rest assured that we aren't going to spend a single moment arguing how many species are endangered or whether global warming is real. Instead, we'll give you three more examples from the summer of 2002 that show the impact of human beings on the environment:

1. Take a look at your cell phone, pager, or laptop computer. One of the elements used in manufacturing its capacitors is coltan, a dull ore mined in the eastern area of the Democratic Republic of Congo. When the demand for coltan skyrocketed a few years ago, thousands of villagers poured into the rain forest to earn $50 a week as miners, five times their average wage elsewhere in the country. With no food infrastructures in place in the rain forest, the new miners ate what they could, slaughtering gorillas and elephants. To power technology, 80 to 90 percent of the lowland gorillas have been killed—there may be as few as two

thousand left in the wild, down from seventeen thousand four years ago.[2]

2. America's emissions standards and water purification efforts have actually improved our environment in the past few decades, but we leave other countries to their own devices. Clouds of pollution over Asian cities are the result of their inattention to the effects of aerosols, burning fossil fuels, millions of inefficient cookers, and open burning of agricultural wastes.

According to U.N. Environment Program chief Klaus Toepfer, however, we cannot ignore what goes on overseas any longer. A major Asian smog cloud isn't staying "over there." Stretching three kilometers high into the atmosphere, scientists estimate that it could travel halfway around the world in a week, cutting the amount of solar energy that reaches the earth, sharply reducing rainfall in some areas and increasing it by as much as 40 percent in others—and it's acid rain. Nobel Laureate Paul Crutzen estimates that up to two million people in India alone die each year from atmospheric pollution.

We share that atmosphere, even if it seems half a world away.[3]

3. The hills of West Virginia are home to some of the clearest, purest streams and rivers in the world. In 1999, Trial Lawyers for Public Justice filed a lawsuit arguing that mountaintop removal mining methods for coal were in violation of the Clean Water Act. A dozen communities had been displaced by the practice of strip mining the hills, then dumping dirt and rock into neighboring valleys. Over five hundred miles of stream had disappeared. Further, environmental studies showed "significant increases in conductivity, hardness, sulfate and selenium (a metal that is toxic at high concentrations) . . . Restricting valley fills . . . will increase the price of coal by only $1 per ton." That translates to just a few cents per month for customers. The Federal judge ruled that such valley fills were illegal.

The lawsuit brought the problem into the public spotlight. The mining companies rallied miners to protest to protect their jobs. Despite input to the Environmental Protection Agency report that an entire ecosystem was being destroyed, in May 2002 Congress passed amendments to the Clean Water Act so that the valley filling could continue.[4]

While politicians debate the evidence on global warming, people everywhere are seeing signs of deteriorating ecosystems. The debates seem irrelevant in view of certain cold hard facts:

- More than one-quarter of America's songbird species are in decline, with perhaps sixty-five million birds dying from pesticides each year.
- More than 40 percent of our lakes and rivers aren't considered safe for swimming. Warnings not to eat fish from local rivers are everywhere.
- Up to 86 percent of the coral reef surrounding Indonesia is dead or dying.
- The Arctic Sea ice thinned from an average of ten feet to less than six in just twenty years.

ARE WE SLEEPING?
Perhaps the facts are so overwhelming that people are numbed, rather than called to action.

We've been lulled into complacency by many things:

- A pause in the energy crisis.
- The endless debate over global warming (when many scientists admit they don't actually have the knowledge to predict what is happening).
- Progress in the United States (Lake Erie no longer catches fire).
- Businesses that meet environmental standards (with no evaluation of whether the standards are adequate).
- Lack of good public transportation that continues the love affair Americans have with their cars despite ever-increasing traffic jams and commute times.
- A knowledge that factories "over there" are creating much more pollution than we are.

If the environmental threats still don't seem real to you, look back at our stories about gorillas and coltan mining, coal mining, and the Asian cloud. These came not from extremist environmental groups but from the Minneapolis *Star Tribune*, Reuters News Service, Bill Moyers, and public television. The problems are too big to hide.

For centuries, humankind has turned its ingenuity to conquering nature. We've climbed the highest peaks, built shelters that let us live in the Antarctic, bested the wildest river rapids, turned deserts into farms, harnessed the wind for power. Somehow we've lost the truth that we are a part of nature. What happens to nature happens to us. Without a new understanding of nature, we may soon find that its unchanging laws are turning against us.

OUR IMAGE OF NATURE

Before suggesting a new master image for our relationship with nature, let's look at how our understanding has evolved.

Nature As God

In ancient times, from Egypt to the Americas, nature was something to be worshiped and appeased. People feared floods, droughts, and hail but also knelt before images of Mother Earth as the source of all life. If you examine the plagues visited on Egypt as Moses convinced Pharaoh to release the Hebrew slaves, each shows the sovereignty of God against Pharaoh's need to appease nature.

Nature As Creation

With the rise of Christianity, nature was separated from the Creator. Both the beauty and the terror of the natural world were recognized, but God was perfect; nature was part of the fall.

Nature As Awesome

Scientists such as Galileo and Kepler, among the first to question the official positions of the church about nature, studied nature to give God the glory for its incredible intricacy. Their work embodied the essence of Romans 1:20, "For since the creation of the world God's invisible qualities—his eternal power and divine nature—have been clearly seen, being understood from what has been made, so that men are without excuse."

Nature As Explainable

However, as the Reformation continued, efforts were concentrated on finding the principles and rules that made the earth tick. The goal was understanding and taming nature so that humankind would control the land, sky, and seas.

Nature As Harnessable

The Age of Exploration fueled this image; new lands rich in untapped resources presented new possibilities and opportunities. As the Industrial Revolution dawned, the transformation was complete. Instead of holding nature in reverence, we viewed it as a vast set of resources to tap for the economic engine of progress. Many looked to the biblical creation story to support this view: "So God created man in his own image, in the image of God he created him; male and female he created them. God blessed them and said to them, 'Be fruitful and increase in number; fill the earth and subdue it.'"[5]

Subdue the earth. The Hebrew words are also translated as "be masters over it" or "have dominion over the earth." These images all suggest that the earth is here to serve our purposes. However, this interpretation ignores the sentence that precedes God's instructions to us: We are created in the image of God. A careful reading of the original Hebrew indicates that the way "subdue" and "image of God" are linked in the same sentence means that the best interpretation is that we are to act toward the earth as God would. We are to care for our earthly home.

Taking care of a garden implies not only coaxing a good harvest out of it this season, but working it in a way that guarantees great harvests in the future. Genesis 2:15 confirms this interpretation: "The LORD God took the man and put him in the Garden of Eden to work it and take care of it." We are to tend to the earth as God would, not subdue it in ways that also destroy what God has created. The choice is clear, for we are subject to the laws of nature:

> The globe doesn't need to be saved by us, and we couldn't kill it if we tried. What we do need to save—and what we have done a fair job of bollixing up so far—is the earth as we like it, with its climate, air, water and biomass all in that destructible balance that best supports life as we have come to know it. Muck that up, and the planet will simply shake us off, as it's shaken off countless species before us. In the end, then, it's us we're trying to save . . ."[6]

That may seem to clash with several centuries of believing that humankind is the pinnacle of God's creation. However, if the verses in Genesis tell us that God placed us here to tend to the garden, then part of being at the top is assuming stewardship for the rest of creation as one of our assignments.

We are stewards of the earth itself, responsible for how we treat it and the condition it is in after we leave. We can't shirk the responsibility that God has given us and then say, "We're God's creation. God will take care of us." God gave us everything we needed here, but we haven't used it as God would have us use it.

Stewards of the earth . . . the idea is starting to gain momentum. Listen to Katherine Sullivan, a three-time space shuttle astronaut:

> Will the immense power of global systems withstand the impact of humanity? Or is it possible that our collective actions will change the nature of our planet enough to cripple its ability to support life?
>
> I no longer believe that we can wait for all the scientific data needed to answer these questions conclusively. We must recognize immediately what it means to be citizens of the planet. It means accepting our obligation to be stewards of the earth's life-giving capacities.[7]

It's time to change our image from subduers to stewards. It's the difference between clear-cut logging and sustaining a forest.

TENDING THE ORCHARD WHILE TAPPING THE TREES

Some friends of ours own acres of sugar maples in Wisconsin. To guarantee the longevity of the sugarbush, or maple orchard, sugarmakers have developed a body of wisdom about caring for the trees. Before a tree is tapped, it must be at least ten inches in diameter—which means it is about forty years old. New tap holes are placed away from old ones. If a tree was defoliated by insects or otherwise stressed, the sugarmaker may not tap it at all. When these principles are followed, the trees remain productive for over a hundred years. Thus a sugarmaker is tending the orchard for the future as well as the present.

However, many things about the process are a mystery. No one knows exactly what causes the sap to flow. There are lots of explanations, but unlike other hardwood trees, the sap in maples moves toward the branches when temperatures freeze and runs down when it thaws. Even without complete understanding of the process, though, sugarmakers have learned how to tap the trees while tending to the orchard. We can do the same with the earth, even without complete understanding of nature.

Tending the earth for the future implies using resources in ways that preserve the environment for our children and grandchildren. Frequently, ideas like this are dismissed with the rationale that alternative energy sources, organic foods, decreased dependency on cars, and other "green" philosophies are too costly to be practical. Betsy Taylor, director of the Center for a New American Dream, asks us to rethink the true cost: "People assume that a so-called sustainable economy means we have to make sacrifices and give up 'the good life,'" says Taylor. "But look what we're already giving up in our current dream: we're losing cultural traditions, indigenous wisdom, species, languages, relationships, trust, community, and health—all things that are precious beyond money."[8]

Further, refusing to give up the "good life" is no different than the way we would ruin our own health if we refused to give up a diet of nothing but chocolate and soda pop. Momentary pleasures would soon give way to lethargy, cavities, and obesity. Neglecting nature, just like neglecting our health, *will* catch up with us.

Our image of the good life is both fueled and sustained by the corporations that grow by keeping us in the consumer mentality. Consumers envision a paradise equipped with the perfect house, the perfect car, convenience food, a wide variety of entertainment to chose from, and a sense of well-being that comes from what we have, the fruits of the acquiring myth. Citizens envision a paradise of clean air, clean water, land that produces foods that are good for us, and a sense of well-being that comes from relationships, the result of believing we have a corporate calling. The choice is ours, but to change a culture nurtured on the acquiring myth, businesses must take a role.

THE ROLE THAT BUSINESS MUST PLAY

While the last hundred years have been more destructive to the earth than all of the rest of human history combined, we are ingenious, and we can turn that creativity toward developing what are becoming known as sustainable practices. As U.N Secretary General Kofi Annan put it, "Without the private sector, sustainable development will remain only a distant dream. We are not asking corporations to do something different from their normal business; we are asking them to do their normal business differently."[9] We want them to learn to tap the trees while tending the orchard, a move toward sustainable development.

Sustainable development means that we take resources at a lower rate than we use them. Right now, we do the opposite—in twelve months we take from the earth a volume of crops, animals, and other biomatter that it takes 14.4 months to replenish. Just like a household budget, you can only run so far into debt. To reverse the trend, we need to get creative and make more than we use.

However, businesses must be at the core of the effort. Why? Here are just a few reasons:

- Because most agriculture is now run by businesses, not small farmers.
- Our infrastructures are based on cars, and citizens on their own cannot change the type of fuel used.
- We can place filters on our water taps, but most of the pollution that finds its way into our lakes and streams comes from industry, not consumers.

Looking at other sources of stress on our environment, if every household in America recycled everything it could, solid waste would only be reduced by 2 percent. The bulk of the problems are rooted in business.

For decades, businesses have fought hard against environmentalists, claiming that tougher pollution control standards and regulations around resource extraction amount to a tax on their goods. The higher prices they must charge makes them less competitive in the world marketplace.

Their arguments have one huge flaw: *The costs to the environment are real, whether reflected in product price or not.* The inefficiencies in the markets result in failure to recognize those costs. This means that consumers might enjoy a lower-priced car or cotton shirt today, but tomorrow they'll pay the true cost—through taxes to fund the cleanup of our water and air, increased waste disposal costs, health care costs due to pollution-related illnesses, and countless other costs hidden by business's ability to shift expenses away from their own bottom line. Neva Goodwin, ecological economist, head of the Global Development and Environment Institute at Tufts University, and an advocate of cost internalization, explains the problem clearly in terms of the economic power of corporations: "Power is largely what externalities are about. What's the point of having power, if you can't use it to externalize your costs—to make them fall on someone else?"[10]

Remember, as our laws currently stand, corporations are beholden to their shareholders. Absent specific regulation, they have no responsibility toward the environment. Yet, if companies are truly operating without conscience, then we have failed miserably as citizens in our complacency as consumers.

To keep the acquiring myth from overwhelming our environment, somehow we have to get corporations to work for the environment. The tremendous innovations and global efforts needed won't happen unless corporations lend their clout to the task. So what do we do?

CHANGING THE RESPONSIBILITIES OF BUSINESS

Paul Hawken, in *The Ecology of Commerce,* simplifies the new paradigm for corporations if they are to accept the mission of stewardship of the earth:

> Business has three basic issues to face: what it takes, what it makes, and what it wastes, and the three are intimately connected. First, business takes too much from the environment and does so in a harmful way; second, the products it makes require excessive amounts of energy, toxins, and pollutants; and finally, the method of manufacture and the very products themselves produce extraordinary waste and cause harm to present and future generations of all species including humans.[11]

A stern indictment, yes, but the evidence is overwhelming that Hawken is right on all three counts.

What Business Takes

America grew on the wings of cheap energy and bountiful resources, but in a very real sense the party is over. When coal companies espouse that mountains and valleys must be leveled to meet our energy needs, we need a new solution. All of us must insist that industries tend to the orchards they control even as they tap the sugar trees.

While the destruction may be most visible in mining and other ore extraction, the problem is much more widespread. Consider the practice of clear-cut logging. Even when corporations follow reforestation principles, they usually replant just one or two different species of trees. The forests lose biodiversity which in turn results in loss of wildlife and depletion of nutrients that the "crop rotation" of a natural forest cycle avoids.

There are alternatives. The Menomonee Tribe of Wisconsin selectively harvests its forests to sustain the ecosystem in its diverse, natural state. Similar projects are arising elsewhere. Appalachian Sustainable Development (ASD) helps interested landowners develop plans for preserving streams, waterways, and wildlife habitats while regenerating biodiversity. Low-quality trees are harvested first, unlike usual logging practices, to make way for better quality timber in the future. ASD purchases harvested trees that meet sustainability standards for use in manufacturing. The landowners need a mindset of tending the orchard, as short-term gains are diminished in favor of long-term income. Yet ASD points out, "The beauty of the process is its affordability. Because of the proximity of trees to their market, and because of the value-adding steps in the process, it is possible to pay a substantial premium to loggers and landowners, while charging only slightly more to the end user."[12]

The issue of what businesses take extends to agriculture as well, where often what is being "taken" is healthy soil. Cotton for example accounts for only 3 percent of worldwide land use but 25 percent of the total pesticides used. Patagonia spent the early 1990s investigating organic agricultural issues and experimenting with organic cotton clothing. In 1996, they announced that all Patagonia cotton clothing would be 100 percent organic or they would stop selling cotton sportswear. To foster employee commitment, "Three hundred of us took tours of cotton fields in California's Central Valley and we saw firsthand the horrible impact of intensive pesticide use. It was an experience that prompted many of us to buy organic food for ourselves and our families."[13] The fields were dotted with ponds of resulting chemical deposits—some agriculturists believe these areas may never again be safe for planting.

Contrast this with the growing practices championed by the organization Navdanya (Nine Seeds) in New Delhi. Navdanya works with farmers in an area for three years. They introduce native plants that can be grown organically using natural fertilizers, without artificial chemicals. The yields of these farmers are similar to neighboring farmers, but the organic farms spend almost 70 percent less for fertilizers, pesticides, and seeds. The investment of three years of learning how produced sustainable harvest methods.

The organizations' founder, Vandana Shiva, developed a passion for local farming as a child. One day, she asked her mother for a polyester dress like the other girls were wearing at school. Her mother said, "If that is what you want, of course you shall have it. But remember, your nylon frock will help a rich man buy a bigger car. And the cotton that you wear will buy a poor family at least one meal." Vandana didn't get the dress, and she never forgot the lesson. Her organization now has spread to some eighty farming districts.[14]

A handful of business people have taken seriously the challenge of reducing what they take through cutting-edge strategies for their own energy needs. Patagonia adhered to its statement of purpose that it "exists as a business to inspire and implement solutions to the environmental crisis" by going with wind energy for 100 percent of its California facilities. Jil Zilligen, director of their environmental programs, said, "The cost of our wind energy reflects what we feel is more the true cost of energy. When we're buying nonrenewables, there are other costs we don't see until later. We still pay for them down the line in the form of higher insurance premiums and cleanup fees—things like that . . . and as resources become more scarce, we see it as giving us more of a competitive advantage in business."[15] Patagonia's distribution center in Nevada relies in part on solar power.

Creativity also leads the search for alternatives to manufacturing petroleum-based plastics. The banana industry has funded research substituting fiber from the stalks of banana plants for nylon. WorldWise distributes garden containers, pet food bowls, and other products made from 90 to 100 percent post-consumer recycled plastic. Patagonia's fleece products are made from recycled pop bottles.

What Businesses Make

Planned obsolescence is something we joke about but are only just beginning to understand its impact on the environment. Old video games don't work on new systems. Computers can't handle software upgrades. New boots don't fit old ski bindings. In a myriad of ways we're encouraged to discard what we have and embrace something new.

"They sure don't make things like they used to" is another way in which businesses are wasteful. Perhaps it's happened to you: a VCR or the CD player in your compact stereo system breaks down. You take the unit to the store and are told, "It'll cost you more to repair it than to buy a new one. We don't even have a repair shop here anymore." It's a system designed to create waste.

Paul Hawken started the successful tool catalog company Smith & Hawken after a farmer showed him a pile of tools that were poorly made: "Handles were broken well up the shaft. That meant the wood was poorly selected first-growth ash. Tanged hoes had been torn away from the ferrule. The shovels had snapped at just about every point from the handle to the socket to the head. The teeth of the rakes were splayed in several directions."[16]

Smith & Hawken began selling tools made in England, where gardeners can count on using the same spade or pitchfork for more than twenty years. And they're making a good profit, even if customers don't have to come back every few years to replace poorly made tools.

Then there are all the clothing and toys and gadgets that aren't meant to be used for more than a few hours. Molded plastic figurines and gadgets from fast-food restaurants. Socks that wear through the heels in a day. Fashions your teenager won't flaunt for more than two weeks. Even furniture. After fifteen years of living with her brother's couch (which he'd used for a dozen years first) Jane finally went to purchase a couch in her favorite color, blue. She was told, "I'm sorry, blue just isn't in fashion now." So much for decorating your home in a color scheme you'll love forever; soon it will be out of style.

Worse are products that are actually hazardous to our environment: items that don't decompose or are classified as hazardous waste.

With all the things we need in the world, such as renewable sources of energy, decent healthcare products, or creative activities that will bring families together, can't businesses find better things to make?

What Businesses Waste

Feel the supple strength of silk fabric. Silkworms spin that thread without producing any toxic waste or using any chemicals. Bees make honey without any additives. Or consider the magnificent production process that results in a giant redwood. There is no waste. Everything eventually is returned to the soil to nourish new living things.

In nature, waste equals food. In our consumer society, just about everything ends up as waste. Over thirty-five billion pounds of toxic waste were generated in 1995, 7 percent more than in 1991. Over seventy-two thousand different industrial chemicals are used by businesses in the United States, excluding foods, drugs, cosmetics, and pesticides. Most of these *have not* been tested for environmental or health concerns.

Consider, too, that our so-called productive agricultural practices aren't at all efficient: We merely substitute fossil fuel for human labor while depleting soil, water, and wildlife.

And that's only the industrial side of waste. The Environmental Protection Agency estimates that each person in the United States manages to toss 1,646 pounds of waste into landfills every year. And while 60 percent of us say we would buy "green," that is, pay more for products if we knew they were less wasteful or more energy efficient, only 15 percent of us actually do when we are faced with opening our pocketbook.[17]

Even though the United States has tougher emission standards than many countries, we still produce more greenhouse gasses than any other country because of the sheer amount of time we spend in our many cars (which now outnumber registered drivers).

The sooner we all start working to tend to this orchard, the only home we have, the better, for the problems will only get worse. As Jane Goodall put it, "I feel deep shame when I look into the eyes of my grandchildren and think how much damage has been done to Planet Earth since I was their age. Each of us must work as hard as we can now to heal the hurts and save what is left."[18]

And businesses must work the hardest.

SIGNS OF HOPE

Many companies are trying, at least harder than before if not hard enough. One of the first companies to voluntarily assume responsibility for the environmental costs of its product was Coors. While they do not claim to have a perfect record on environmental issues, they were early pioneers in two areas:

- *Recycling.* Coors took the lead in both developing aluminum cans and the recycling programs needed to protect the environment.
- *Water treatment.* Coors designed and built the first modern wastewater treatment plant in Colorado in 1959, decades before regulations required it.

In the ten years ended in 2002, Coors cut its annual generation of hazardous waste from regular activities by more than 90 percent.

Similarly, in 1975, 3M began its 3P program—"Pollution Prevention Pays." Rather than controlling emissions or safely disposing of waste, they determined to change their processes so the pollutants were not produced in the first place. Since then, through more than forty-seven hundred projects worldwide, 3M's employees have reduced pollutants used in manufacturing, redesigned products and equipment to be less wasteful, and developed better recycling methods. Besides preventing 807,000 tons of pollutants, they estimate corporate savings of $827 million. In 1986, they set a goal of reducing 90 percent of their emissions by the year 2000.

3M has willingly taken hits to its bottom line as well, to be faithful to its environmental stance. In May 2000, it voluntarily ceased manufacturing Scotchguard, a forty-year-old fabric treatment product with $300 million in annual sales. Their own tests showed that the compound didn't decompose in the environment.[19] Another company that is now trying is Monsanto. Pummeled by environmentalists over their commitment to genetically modified plants, Robert Shapiro, the former CEO, said, "We've learned that there is often a very fine line between scientific confidence on the one hand and corporate arrogance on the other . . . It was natural for us to see this as a scientific issue. We didn't listen very well to people who insisted that there were relevant ethical, religious, cultural, social, and economic issues as well."[20]

In 2000, Monsanto committed to operating under a new pledge to listen more, consider broad ramifications of their actions, and be responsible leaders. They report annually their results with regard to the elements of the pledge—dialogue, transparency, respect, sharing, and benefits—so that they are held responsible. Current president Hendrik Verfaillie wrote, "We have approached the Pledge not as a list of activities or a normal corporate initiative, but as a mandate to change our behavior."[21] Are they perfect? No, but they are publishing safety data summaries on their biotech products on the Internet and working with advisory councils. They expanded their commitments to social responsibility after operating under the Pledge for a year.

As these companies work to change their practices, they are in effect changing their paradigm of nature, acknowledging that there are limits to our ability to harness nature. Perhaps that shift is the impetus behind the popularity of Daniel Quinn's book *Ishmael*.

Ishmael starts with a simple ad: "Teacher seeks pupil. Must have an earnest desire to save the world. Apply in person."[22] The teacher turns out to be a gorilla who slowly, painstakingly helps his pupil see how humankind is different from all other species. Humans believe they know better than God how to run the planet—and they're destroying it. Ishmael divides the inhabitants of the earth into two categories: "Leavers—those who live in the hands of the gods" and "Takers—those who have taken the whole world out of the hands of the gods."

It's a gripping book, sort of a glimpse of how a cultural anthropologist from another planet might view our culture. And it's a bit frightening as you realize that our civilization assumes that we are immune from the laws of nature.

But we aren't. We haven't found a fountain of youth. We need food and rest. We can't escape the pull of gravity or the forces of inertia. When we deny that we are part of nature, eventually it catches up with us. Put another way, we have a choice: we can continue to act like Takers and assume that we can run the earth. Or we can become Leavers and discern God's wisdom for how to interact with nature.

Where were you when I laid the earth's foundation?
Tell me, if you understand.
Who marked off its dimension? Surely you know!
Who stretched a measuring line across it?
On what were its footings set, or who laid its cornerstone—
while the morning stars sang together
and all the angels shouted for joy?[23]

TOP-DOWN SOLUTIONS
FOR THE EARTH

Slowly but surely, models for sustainable business and manufacturing practices are emerging that follow the model of tapping the trees while tending the orchard. Perhaps most important, these businesses are finding that these practices are green in two ways: Not only are they environmentally sound, but they are profitable! By applying creativity and ingenuity, they are finding ways to harmonize with nature that actually increase revenues or decrease costs.

What businesses need are incentives to change—environmental and monetary incentives. Otherwise, the forces of inertia rally around the cries of "It will be too expensive or time-consuming or difficult to redesign or retool or re-envision our products or processes." We can think of at least two incentives.

First, eventually the changes will be forced upon businesses, whether because of regulation, consumer activism, or depletion of resources. The costs of being reactive rather than proactive are skyrocketing; remember McDonald's restaurants and the protests about chickens? McDonald's poured money into defending the conditions under which chickens for their restaurants were raised. Then it had to buckle under to activists and procure chickens raised under more humane conditions, increasing its costs. Further, the battle brought all of their operations under higher public scrutiny.

Second, companies that have already changed what they take, make, and waste have frequently found that when all the dust settles, their bottom line is stronger. Here are some of the strategies they have followed.

CLOSED-LOOP MANUFACTURING

Coors' development of aluminum cans and recycling, with the idea that they would reduce the amount of waste they created, was one of the early examples of manufacturers taking responsibility for the waste their products create both at the beginning *and* at the end of their life cycles.

Europe has led the way in making companies responsible for their products once consumers are through with them. In the Netherlands, car buyers pay an additional "disassembly tax" when they purchase their vehicle. When the car reaches the end of its useful life, they take it to an auto disassembly plant,

> where it is carefully stripped of anything that can still be used. Then only the metal shell is crushed and recycled (in the United States everything—wires, plastic, and so forth—just gets crushed, and a large percentage is simply lost as waste). The Dutch plants, which are cheap and low-tech, employ many workers and take any cars. The disassembly tax is part of the Dutch National Environmental Policy Plan (or "Green Plan") and will soon be extended to include many other consumer goods.[24]

These kinds of policies have an impact on how the vehicles are designed in the first place. For example, BMW reduced the number of different types of plastic used in one of its vehicles from over twenty to just four so that it would be easier (and less costly) to recycle.

The difficulties the electronics industry faces show the importance of nationwide coordination of such efforts. Computers, cell phones, televisions, and other consumer goods contain lead, copper, mercury, plastic, and other recyclable and/or hazardous substances. So far, efforts at recycling have been piecemeal. Best Buy Company sponsored ten electronics recycling events in 2001 and several more in 2002. California considered legislation for recycling fees to be added to the purchase price—$10 per computer or television, but surveys showed that consumers balk at paying the true life-cycle cost of a product, from manufacturing to recycling.

The National Electronic Product Stewardship Initiative was formed in 2001, with representatives from government, industry, and conservation advocacy groups. Their goal is to design a feasible nationwide program, which is taking longer than the original projection of a yearlong effort. At issue is determining how to spread the cost and finding viable recycling processes, which so far are too labor intensive. In short, the issues are complicated, but two things bear repeating:

1. A better solution than recycling is to not produce any more than necessary in the first place. Attention to the benefits of closed-loop manufacturing and durable goods would lessen the need.
2. Since consumers enjoy the benefits of the products, shouldn't they bear as much responsibility for the stewardship of electronic products as the manufacturers, retailers, and government agencies involved? Yet, consumers can't make informed decisions if market prices do not reflect true costs.

Many innovative solutions are being researched—Sony has suggested that electronic equipment be "mined." A single abandoned surface mine could hold seventy-two billion computers. Improved ore-processing technology could then be used to extract materials such as copper, gold, iron, glass, and plastic the equipment contains. Electronic waste is actually richer in copper content than copper ore. "The key is to put the material in place in large quantities and then process it," says Mark Small, vice president of Corporate Environment, Safety and Health for Sony in San Diego.[25] Costs would be offset by commercial value of the recycled goods and decreased landfill costs.

Sound crazy? Or is it a better solution than simply dumping outdated equipment, with its lead, copper, and plastic intact, into landfills as we currently do? Perhaps a significant reason that Sony is a leader in seeking a solution to this problem is that landfill fees in Japan are between $300 to $400 a ton, compared with $20 to $30 in the United States. In other words, Sony is already coming to terms with the true cost of obsolete electronics and anticipates being held responsible for what they make.

PRODUCE SERVICES, NOT GOODS

Do you *need* to own a refrigerator or do you simply *want* to keep food chilled and fresh? Do you *need* to own carpeting or do you simply *want* to cover your floors? How many things would you be content not to buy if you didn't have to? Several companies asked this question and are changing from a product orientation to providing services.

One of the best-known innovators in this orientation shift is Ray Anderson, chair of Interface in Atlanta. They now lease floor covering. As described by Amory Lovins, author of *Natural Capitalism,*

> You'll pay me a little bit every month for a tax deductible operating lease, under which I will promise that every month my little elves will come in the night, look at your carpet, take away the worn one square meter of carpet tiles, immediately replace them with fresh ones. I won't need to disturb your operations because the worn bits are not under the furniture, and 80 percent or 90 percent of the wear is on 10 percent or 20 percent of the area, so I'm only going to replace this with a fifth as much carpet as if I had to replace everything, whether it's worn or not.[26]

Are jobs lost? No. Net employment went up because of increased service jobs. Interface doubled its revenue in the first four years of its "floor surface leasing." Now the company has gone on to develop carpeting made of renewable materials rather than petroleum products. Between its recycling of old carpet, the need to only replace a small percentage, and processes that use less material, it has reduced by 97 percent the total materials used in its manufacturing plants.

Other services being leased include elevators and solvents. Schindler owns the elevators it manufactures and covers the operating and repair costs while leasing a "vertical transportation service." Dow and Safety Clean deliver solvents, then repurify the solutions after factories are done with them. The process can be repeated fifty to a hundred times and the factories don't have to deal with disposal of hazardous waste.

Leasing services is a success story that makes reduce, reuse, recycle a meaningful mantra. When we start thinking about things in terms of the services they provide rather than as something we have to own, the possibilities are endless.

LEAD THE WAY

Another leader is Patagonia. Founder Yvon Chouinard's goal for the company from the start was to do the right thing for the environment, not to make huge profits. Besides switching to organic cotton, they've successfully led campaigns for dam removal; employees are granted paid leaves of up to two months to work for environmental groups; and they pay bail for any employees arrested during "green" demonstrations or protests.

Why are we mentioning companies like Patagonia and The Body Shop again and again? Because corporate responsibility—stewardship—is part of their mission, and they're accomplishing it. There are few examples of environmentalists within businesses because it is so difficult to effect change from within the system. In writing *In Earth's Company*, Carl Frankel looked for authentic environmental champions within the corporate world. The three that he located had all been fired by the time the book came out.

However, the impact of corporate leadership by companies with the clout of Patagonia, The Body Shop, and others can be huge. We need more of them—more companies that form with the message to shareholders that they will not be the only beneficiaries of the company.

CREATE LOCAL SYSTEMS

When tomatoes are only being shipped to a local market, they can be picked ripe and juicy, not hard and green. And they can be bred for tender skins, not tough ones that can withstand being trucked across the country.

When local conditions are the basis for agricultural practices, building designs, or transportation systems, the environmental savings can be enormous. Australian architect Glen Murkatt will only build in Australia, where he understands the weather and the land because "his houses are very site-specific. The architect doesn't know the site just by sight; he studies the prevailing breezes, the water drainage and the flora and fauna of each proposed building spot."[27] With moving glass panels, louvered blinds, and thermal shades, the owner can "adjust" the house to the weather at considerable energy savings.

ELIMINATE REWARDS IN CURRENT ECONOMY FOR SHORT-TERM EXPLOITATION

Our current economic system rewards companies for extracting trillions of tons of resources from the earth and then throwing away over 90 percent of it as waste. There are alternatives that *will not* break the backs of industry but will instead properly place costs so that companies are incented to change and consumers are aware of the true costs of what they buy.

Richard Sandor, the CEO and founder of Environmental Financial Products, based in Chicago, has networked American, Canadian, and Mexican firms to form the Chicago Climate Exchange, launched in 2003. Companies are able to trade permits to emit greenhouse gasses—the less you emit, the more you can sell to others. "The power of the free market is that it can restore nature's wealth as it increases financial wealth," Sandor says.[28] A similar market has already lessened sulfur emissions.

Another side of the economic issue is "buying green." While early recycled products were both more costly and inferior to regular items, this is no longer true. Further, the influence of one or two large buyers can influence industry, as was demonstrated in 1985 when Ralph Nader convinced the government's General Services Administration to order five thousand air-bag equipped cars. Ford won the bid and other manufacturers soon offered the option.

We can concentrate that kind of buyer's clout to shape environmental practices. Hospitals, among other businesses, have formed Group Purchasing Organizations. One of these GPO's represents eighteen hundred hospitals and healthcare organizations. Three of the biggest support environmentally preferable purchasing, minimizing use of products containing latex, polyvinyl chloride, mercury, and chlorine. "They're big enough to not just signal the market, but move the market. The goal isn't simply products that are less toxic, but totally nontoxic. And it's our job to help the professionals see the connection between taking a patient's temperature [the mercury thermometer] and a tuna fish swimming in the ocean 2,000 miles away," says Charlotte Brody, executive director of Health Care Without Harm.[29]

BE SELF-ACTUATED, NOT DRIVEN BY REGULATIONS

Progress is being made, but we still have a long way to go as evidenced by the World Summit on Sustainable Development in 2002. Distracted by problems in the Middle East, President Bush refused to join the heads of state from over a hundred countries at the ten-day meeting. And Colin Powell only came for the last two days. Jeers and cat-calls from the audience accompanied his speech, in protest of the obvious lack of commitment by the United States to the process of joining the world to address the areas of water, energy, health, agriculture, and biodiversity.

Steve Sawyer of Greenpeace said of the conference, "It's a clear victory for the Americans, the Saudis, the OPEC nations and every country that is against transforming the worldwide energy supply in the direction of sustainable development. That's the worst possible conclusion we could have had because it's no conclusion at all."[30]

On the other hand, in contrast to the 1992 Summit in Rio, the nongovernment organizations (NGO's) were officially considered part of the meetings and influenced the issues the media covered. And several chemical company associations formed partnerships during the meeting with NGOs: The World Chlorine Council partnered with World Vision to improve water and sanitation in Ghana, Mali, and Niger; the International Council of Chemical Associations joined with the World Wildlife Association to rebuild infrastructures; and there were others.

While scientists and governments and corporations argue about global warming and responsibility and costs, the earth is calling to be cared for. Corporations must start thinking of being responsible not to current environmental laws, but to the laws that will evolve as more people grasp the true state of the economy. Nature is neither fully controllable nor fully understandable. Neither is the sap run in the sugarbush. Just as the sugarmakers have learned to tap the trees while tending to the long-term health of their orchards, we can learn to leave the earth in God's hands, caring for it as stewards of the One who created us as part of and dependent on the wonderful world we call home.

*I consider that our present sufferings are not worth comparing
with the glory that will be revealed in us. The creation waits
in eager expectation for the sons of God to be revealed.
For the creation was subjected to frustration,
not by its own choice, but by the will of the one
who subjected it, in hope that the creation itself
will be liberated from its bondage to decay
and brought into the glorious freedom of the children of God.*
　　—Romans 8:18-21

BOTTOM-UP STRATEGIES
FOR OUR PLANET

*Only when emphasis is placed on humanitarian values
that affect the welfare and happiness of all will the land be safe,
and only when we realize that the real dividends lie
in the realm of the imponderables will we do
what is necessary to restore what has been despoiled
and protect what is left.*
　　—Sigurd F. Olson[31]

What would you be giving up to use any of the following? Consider especially what each might subtract from what Sigurd Olson refers to as the "imponderables."

- A household cleaning product you can drink safely.
- An inkjet printer cartridge that can be refilled and reused.
- A shirt made from cotton fibers grown without chemicals.
- A car that emits water as its only waste product.

All of these things exist. The higher we value imponderables such as wilderness, environment, and tending the orchard while tapping the trees, the more desire we will have to seek these alternatives for ourselves. Look at the opening words of Psalm 24:

The earth is the Lord's,
and everything in it, the world,
and all who live in it[32]

God gave us charge of everything in this world. Perhaps in no other stewardship is our individual role so clear: The choices we make and the tenderness we show toward our environment determine the kind of world our children and grandchildren will inherit. We are stewards of their inheritance. Yet within the systems of our planet lies the wisdom to tend to it as God intended. Remember that the world is God's and that we can use God-given wisdom to care for it.

We're starting to learn from nature, where spiders spin webs with fibers as strong as Kevlar without a single drop of toxic chemicals. For a hundred years or more, the ease of applying technology to manufacturing kept us from using our ingenuity. While we've given several examples of companies that are reversing that trend, the faster we change our ways, the faster the earth can begin to recover.

While the problems are global in size, it will take every one of us—what we buy, what we throw away, what we call attention to— to get corporations to change. But first, it seems that many of us need to grasp that we're part of the problem before we can be effective agents for change.

Besides the media images of environmental extremists, some very real factors have discouraged people from turning "green": cost, convenience, and complacency.

Cost

A recent college graduate pointed out, "I came out of school with an incredible awareness of environmental problems, but I have thousands of dollars in school loans. So rather than raging at the beast I have to get employed by the beast. And, while I want to buy from organic growers because their produce looks five times as tasty as the stuff in stores, I can't afford it on my entry level salary."

The price differentials are changing, but even more important, remember that we're bearing the costs in different ways—sixty-five million songbirds lost each year due to our agribusiness practices. Taxes to cover cleanup costs. Perhaps even our medical bills as we learn more about the impact of the fertilizers and pesticides used so freely on crops.

In moving from consumer to citizen, each of us has to evaluate the true cost of each thing we buy and decide when and how we're going to pay the real price.

Convenience

Much of the merchandise in our stores is designed to save us time (or at least to look like it will save us time). It's easy to fall into the trap of convenience foods in wasteful packaging or disposable products so we don't have to care for them or cheap items that won't last as long.

Further, it takes time to investigate which purchases are better for the environment. At first, setting out to find organic cotton or fair trade coffee or recycled paper goods can seem like a futile treasure hunt. Often we don't even hear much about the alternatives because they're competing with well-known brands backed by huge advertising budgets. But the environmental costs of convenience are too high to pay.

Fortunately, things are changing—due to consumer demands. More and more grocery stores stock organic produce (and there are now standards for being able to use the "organic" label). Wasteful packaging practices are on the wane. And the more we demand change, the more it will happen. Being "green" will become more and more convenient.

Complacency

The environment is such a huge issue that it's easy to become complacent or to assume that the worries belong to businesses or the government. However, if you clip related articles from your local newspaper for a few weeks or surf the Web for a few minutes, you'll probably find enough problems in your own backyard to stir you into action.

THE NEW "THREE R'S"

The slogan of "Reduce, Reuse, Recycle" is a great starting place for individual consumers, but to influence the place where you work, we have a new slogan: "Research, Recommend, and Rally."

Research

First, read for your own awareness. Discover for yourself the story of Sally Fox and Natural Cotton Colours. Understand the Fair Trade movement. Check out *Natural Capitalism* from the library or do a Web search on Amory Lovins and the Rocky Mountain Institute. These are all positive examples that demonstrate how we can change the way we do business.

Second, find the stories that are relevant to your own company. A phenomenal number of corporations and businesses are still unaware that adopting sound environmental practices can be cost-effective. The good news is that the companies that have made this discovery are touting their successes all over their Web sites. Because dollars and cents speak to management, start researching the cost savings other companies in your industry are recognizing.

Recommend

Again, start at the individual level. Begin networking with friends and neighbors, finding cost-effective places and products to buy "green" in your area. Pass on the reasons behind the convictions you've developed and you won't be seen as a fanatic.

Consider donating fair trade coffee for the social hour at your place of worship. Post a little sign that explains how it benefits growers. Carpool with a friend if you need to drive a little farther to purchase items that are environmentally preferable.

Then, look for ways to encourage your office to change its practices. You can start with the easier items, such as switching to recycled computer paper and other office products. The city of Santa Monica investigated using safe rather than toxic cleaning products and quickly switched to nontoxic ones in fifteen of seventeen categories. The total cost was 5 percent less. Brian Johnson, manager of their environmental programs, says, "Green procurement provides cost savings, is easily implementable, and enhances public health and the environment. Some of these purchases are simply no-brainers. If you have a choice between a carcinogenic bathroom cleaner and one that isn't, I can't imagine not choosing the safe alternative."[33]

Find out which office furniture companies use fabrics that need to be disposed of as toxic waste and which use ones that can be turned into mulch for organic farming. Supporting the latter will encourage more manufacturers to adopt "natural capitalism" practices. Do what you can to direct the combined power of your company's dollars toward environmentally sound purchasing.

Rally

Finally, find allies in this effort. Never underestimate the power of a group of citizens or companies to influence corporate America.

At your own company, look for like-minded souls in other departments. Arm them with your research on cost savings from eliminating waste before it is even produced at other corporations in your industry; on discoveries you've made about supply purchases; and on any advances in "natural capitalism" technologies that apply to your firm. The changes may seem unbearably slow, but already the effects of what *Good to Great* refers to as the flywheel effect are being seen.

Flywheels are huge, heavy, and tough to get moving. At first your mighty pushes only inch it forward, but the second rotation is a little easier, and the next rotation is a little faster, "Then, at some point—breakthrough! The momentum of the thing kicks in in your favor, hurling the flywheel forward, turn after turn . . . whoosh! . . . its own heavy weight working for you."[34] Each effort you make is a push to increase your company's awareness of the environmental choices it faces.

At least four forces are already working on that flywheel. One is the momentum being created by events like the World Summit in Johannesburg. The issues are more and more before our eyes. The second is the growing gravity of the situation—the Asian pollution cloud and other environmental catastrophes are too big to hide. Third, the cost savings to be realized are big enough to grab the attention of big business. Fourth is the sheer pressure that groups can bring. Listen to the figures:

- There are thirty-seven hundred colleges and universities in the United States. Together, they spend about $300 billion on supplies. Do you think they have clout if they banded together and insisted on changes in the products they use? Rutgers University has watched its procurement costs drop by 2.4 percent, unadjusted for inflation, over the past ten years due to its efforts in green purchasing.[35]
- Federal, state and local governments spend even more— about $385 billion each year. Massachusetts, which has a director of state sustainability, bought $68 million in recycled goods in 2001.[36]

  Remember the story of the medical supply companies who banded together for purchasing? Other groups can do the same thing to put pressure on industry to change their practices.

As you "Reduce, Reuse, Recycle" and "Research, Recommend, and Rally," remember that the problems are personal. It's our only home that we're trying to save. We're trying to increase the number of Leavers in the world, people who understand that God knows best how to care for the earth; our job is to tend the garden for future generations.

[S]tanding alone on the mountaintop it is easy to realize
that whatever special nests we make—
leaves and moss like the marmots and birds, or tents or piled stone—
we all dwell in a house of one room—
the world with the firmament for its roof . . .
  —John Muir[37]

CHAPTER 8

LOOKING FORWARD
TO LOOKING BACK

EVERYONE'S CALLING

So it is not easy for us to change. But it is possible.
And it is our glory as human beings. . . .
I wonder, if we in the United States were to concentrate—
as our overwhelmingly major priority—
on making ourselves the best possible society we can be,
whether the nations of the world might once again,
without any pressure except the influence of example,
begin to emulate us.[1]
　　—M. Scott Peck, *The Different Drum: Community Making*
　　　and Peace

TAKE A LOOK AT TODAY'S PAPER. HOW DOES THE HEADLINE read? Does it create enthusiasm or dread for the future? Joy or despair?

At the end of the first chapter, we asked what kinds of headlines you'd like to read in the future—ones that shout of more disasters or ones that point toward a bright future for our children and our children's children?

Part of your answer may depend on what time you think it is. As in, what time is it in the history of humankind?

Just about all of us agree on a few things. This is an age of uncertainty. It's the dawn of a new millennium. But, ask people, "If the history of humankind were to span a single day, what time would it be now?" You'll get very different answers.

Some people will tell you, "It's morning." For this group, time stretches out before us indefinitely. So, it's time for business as usual. Perhaps these people believe in God, perhaps they don't. Either way, their everyday lives don't involve checking the eternal calendar to see if the end of the age might be approaching. They feel no rush to work toward a corporate calling, no need to escape the acquiring myth.

Others cry, "It's almost midnight!" They believe that this is the end of the age as Jesus described it. Earthquakes, typhoons, unrest in the Middle East all suggest to them that Jesus's return is imminent. Our time is nearly done. Business doesn't matter because we need to concentrate on our souls, not our corporate calling.

In both cases, faith is almost irrelevant to work. Yet, there's another view, one that acknowledges Jesus's words, "Therefore keep watch, because you do not know the day or the hour."[2] If we aren't sure what time it is, then it's time to get working. Perhaps we have enough time to fulfill our corporate calling, to become stewards as God envisioned in the story of creation.

None of us work to change ourselves without personal motivation. What strikes closest to home for you? Escaping the clutches of the acquiring myth? Working toward social justice? Being able to drink once again from nature's streams? Helping others find meaning and purpose?

Now, imagine that as you close this book, you pray that God will show you how you can live out your corporate calling. Perhaps someday, you'd be able to show an encyclopedia entry like the one below to your children or grandchildren or young adults that look to you as a mentor and say, "I was a part of this."

Corporate-calling revolution, a term used to describe the process of change from an industrial, mechanistic model of business to one based on discovering the true calling of business. In the first years of the twenty-first century, groups of concerned citizens formed throughout the world, drawn together by common concerns about corporate scandals, escalating conflict in the Mideast, and environmental crises. Realizing that the most powerful entities in the world—corporations—were both responsible for and the only hope for resolving these grave events, the movement called for sweeping corporate reforms along five fronts:

1. To ensure that the interests of corporations and of the human race were intertwined, a rechartering of all corporations, with the stipulation that the statement of purpose be linked to the public good (the calling of Purpose).

2. To ensure that business profits do not come at the expense of other stakeholders, a change in business incorporation laws to read "The directors and officers of a corporation shall exercise their powers and discharge their duties with a view to the interests of the corporation and of the shareholders, *but not at the expense of the environment, human rights, the public safety, the communities in which the corporation operates, or the dignity of its employees* (the calling of Profits).

3. To foster cooperation and human rights worldwide, an acknowledgment that unbridled free market policies have transferred wealth and power into the hands of a privileged few. Principles such as the common heritage of natural resources, the need for market regulation to protect the interests of the unprivileged, and the return of political power and free speech to the people became the basis for new market ideologies (the calling of Products and Places).

4. With the combination of greed and lack of meaning finally recognized as the core root of crime, drug abuse, disintegration of the family, and the horrors of sweatshop conditions worldwide, the movement sought to end the destructive forces of a consumption-based economy. A call for meaning and purpose, as well as an emphasis on the interconnectedness of all of humankind transformed the values system that determined workforce patterns (the calling of People).

5. To stop the abuse of the environment, consumer groups wielded their buying power to convince corporations to change. With growing evidence of widespread ecological breakdown, and with incentive under the new charter laws, corporations quickly

responded to calls to adopt the principles of sustainability. Concerns over possible economic slowdowns were soon drowned in a flood of burgeoning creativity that resulted in widespread closed-loop manufacturing, discontinuation of carbon-based fuels, and production processes that mimicked the nonwasteful patterns found in nature (the calling of our Planet).

The ideas were so simple, the evidence supporting the need so compelling, that within five years the movement had become a revolution, ushering in the longest period of sustained peace and prosperity in history.

Sound impossible? Remember, the alternative is the other set of headlines: more corporate fraud, more conflict between the haves and the have-nots, more ecological problems, more breakdown in our families and communities. Whether you join in trying to work toward a better future perhaps depends on your view of time . . . or does it?

If you believe that it's evening, you might consider encouraging business toward a new vision as an evangelism tool for these end times.

If you believe that it's morning, or that God isn't watching, then you might consider which future you want for your children and grandchildren. And you might ask yourself what you'll say when they wonder, "You were alive then and you didn't do anything? Why?"

If you believe that it's midday, then there is a ponderous amount of work ahead of us, work that is a part of our calling. When the owner of the garden returns, you can work toward hearing, "Well done, good and faithful servant. You did all that you could with what you had." That is all God asks.

Yes, changing the world seems impossible, but as Dee Hock put it, "It is far too late and things are far too bad for pessimism."[3]

Start by telling others what you now know about reenvisioning the calling of business. Form a circle for discussion at your church or office.

Help each other discover your assignments.

Keep a vision in front of you of the future you want to see.

And remember, with our God, we are able to do far more than we can ever ask or imagine. Our charge is to do what we are called to do with what we have.

NOTES

Chapter 1

1. John 10:10.
2. Ps. 84:12.
3. Ps. 106:3
4. Eccl. 3:12-13.
5. Baltimore Catechism.
6. Eccl. 5:10-12 (NLT).
7. This story can be found in Luke 12:16-21.
8. Gen. 1:1.
9. Matt. 7:12.
10. Mark 2:27.
11. Matt. 18:21-22.
12. Gen. 2:15.
13. Mark 13:33-37.
14. Beacon Press.
15. From "A Survey of Multinationals: Everybody's Favorite Monsters," *The Economist*, (March 27, 1993), S17. As referenced in David Korten, *When Corporations Rule the World*, 2nd ed. (San Francisco: Barrett-Koehler Publishers, Inc., 2001), 210.
16. Korten, *When Corporations Rule the World*, 210.
17. Benjamin R. Barber, *Jihad vs. McWorld: How Globalism and Tribalism Are Reshaping the World* (New York: Ballantine Books, 1996).
18. James C. Collins and Jerry I. Porras, *Built to Last: Successful Habits of Visionary Companies* (San Francisco: HarperBusiness, 1994).
19. Ian Mitroff and Elizabeth A. Denton, *A Spiritual Audit of Corporate America: A Hard Look at Spirituality, Religion, and Values in the Workplace* (San Francisco: Jossey-Bass Publishers, 1999), 6.

Chapter 2

1. Joseph Campbell, with Bill Moyers, edited by Betty Sue Flowers, *The Power of Myth*. (New York: Doubleday, 1988), 123.
2. Campbell, *The Power of Myth*, xv.
3. Amanda Ripley, "The Night Detective," *Time* (December 30, 2002), 45.
4. Miles Horton, *The Long Haul: An Autobiography*. With Judith Kohl and Herbert Kohl (New York: Teachers College Press, 1998), 149-50.
5. Kise, Stark, and Sandra Krebs Hirsh, *LifeKeys: Who You Are, Why You're Here, What You Do Best* (Bloomington, Minn.: Bethany House Publishers, 1996).
6. Robert Quinn, *Deep Change* (San Francisco: Jossey-Bass, 1996), 158.
7. Peter Block, *The Answer to How Is Yes: Acting on What Matters* (San Francisco: Barrett-Koehler Publishers, Inc., 2002).
8. Ibid., 85
9. Matt. 13:31-32.

Chapter 3

1. From *Back to Methuselah* (1921), as quoted in *The Oxford Dictionary of Phrase, Sayings, and Quotations,* Elizabeth Knowles, ed. (Oxford: Oxford University Press, 1997), 221.
2. J. Scott Armstrong, "Social Irresponsibility in Management," *Journal of Business Research* 5 (1977), 185-213, as referenced in Lynn Sharpe Paine, *Value Shift* (New York: McGraw-Hill, 2003), 150-51.
3. Collins and Porras, *Built to Last,* 47.
4. http://www.jnj.com/our_company/our_credo_history/index.htm (accessed September 6, 2002).
5. Ibid.
6. Adapted from Matt. 25:15-29.
7. David heard Tachi Kiuchi, chairman of Mitsubishi Electric America, speak on what he's learned from trips to the rain forest with other business executives. The ideas can be found in Tachi Kiuchi and Bill Shiremen, *What We Learned in the Rain Forest: Business Lessons from Nature* (San Francisco: Jossey-Bass, 2002).
8. Mike's story is told in Po Bronson, *What Should I Do with My Life* (New York: Random House, 2003).
9. http://www.edwardjones.com/cgi/getHTML.cgi?page=/USA/aboutEJ/index.html (accessed February 27, 2003).
10. Arie De Geus, *The Living Company* (Boston: Harvard Business School Press, 1997), 175.
11. Collins and Porras, *Built to Last,* 7.
12. Kevin Freiberg and Jackie Freiberg, *Nuts! Southwest Airlines' Crazy Recipe for Business and Personal Success* (Austin, Tex.: Bard Press, 1996), 211.
13. Jon Birger, "30-Year Super Stocks: *Money Magazine* Finds the Best Stocks of the Past 30 Years," *Money* (October 9, 2002).
14. Personal interview, September 2002.
15. http://www.worldwise.com/worguidprin.html (accessed September 24, 2002).
16. http://www.worldwise.com/whoweare1.html (accessed September 24, 2002).
17. http://www.sustainableharvest.com/coffee_business_1.htm (accessed September 24, 2002).
18. Defining Quality (Patagonia, Inc., 1998), 29.
19. Holly Welling, "Patagonia: Small World View of Big Business," *Apparel Industry Magazine* 60, no. 12 (1999), AS26-32.
20. http://www.andersenwindows.com/corporate/mission.asp?p=40600000 (accessed October 23, 2002).
21. De Geus, *The Living Company,* 176.
22. Medtronic 2002 Annual Report, 1.
23. This story can be found in Num. 13:1—14:38.
24. Num. 14:8 (NIV).
25. New York: HarperCollins Publishers, Inc., 2001.
26. Ibid, 98.
27. Leonard Sweet, *SoulSalsa* (Grand Rapids, Mich.: Zondervan Publishing House, 2000), 20.
28. Paul Hawken, *Growing a Business* (New York: Fireside Books, 1987), 61.
29. Derek Bok, *The Cost of Talent: How Executives and Professionals Are Paid and How It Affects America* (New York: Free Press, 1993), 108-11, as quoted in *When Corporations Rule the World,* 224.
30. Peter Senge, Art Kleiner, Charlotte Roberts, Richard Ross, George Roth, Bryan Smith, *The Dance of Change: The Challenges to Sustaining Momentum in Learning Organizations* (New York: Doubleday Currency, 1999), 492.
31. John Sherrill and Elizabeth Sherrill, *Glimpses of His Glory* (Wheaton, Ill.: Tyndale House, Inc., 1990), 53.
32. Studs Terkel, *My American Century* (New York: New Press, 1997), 303.
33. Rom. 12:2.
34. Renay's full story is told in Renay Poirier, with Jane Kise, *I Once Was Blind* (Dallas: SunCreek Books, 2003).

35. Copyright © 2002 The American-Israeli Cooperative. http://www.us-israel.org/jsource/biography/schindler.html (accessed October 11, 2002).
36. Emilie Schindler, *Where Light and Shadow Meet: A Memoir* (New York: W.W. Norton & company, Inc., 1990), 94.
37. Margaret Wheatley, *Turning to One Another: Simple Conversations to Restore Hope to the Future* (San Francisco: Barrett-Koehler Publishers, Inc., 2002), 19.

Chapter 4
1. As quoted in *The Oxford Dictionary of Phrase, Sayings, & Quotations* (New York: Oxford University Press, 1997), 469.
2. Kenneth D. Campbell, "Malden Mills Owner Applies Religious Ethics to Business." *MIT Tech Talk*, Cambridge, Mass., April 16, 1997.
   http://web.mit.edu/newsoffice/tt/1997/apr16/4350.html (accessed January 16, 2003).
3. Helen Mintz Belitsky, "Portrait: Aaron Feuerstein" *Hadassah*. http://www.Hadassah.org/news/pub2_14.htm (accessed January 16, 2003).
4. Joan Bavaria, "Democracy, Accountability and the Market System," Trillium Asset Management quarterly newsletter. http://www.trilliuminvest.com/pages/news (accessed September 25, 2002).
5. Milton Friedman, "The Social Responsibility of Business Is to Increase Its Profits," *New York Times Magazine* 33 (September 13, 1970), 122-26.
6. Robert C. Hinkley, "How Corporate Law Inhibits Social Responsibility," *The Humanist* 62, no. 2 (2002), 26.
7. As cited in Belitsky, "Portrait: Aaron Feuerstein" (see ch. 4, n. 3). The verse is found in Deut. 24:14 (NIV).
8. Matt. 7:24-27 (NIV).
9. http://news.bbc.co.uk/1/hi/business/1217716.stm (accessed January 18, 2003).
10. Jim Collins, "The Secret Life of the CEO: Is the Economy Just Built to Flip?" *Fast Company*. http://pf/fastcompany.com/online/63/secretlife2.html (October 13, 2002).
11. William White, CEO, Wedge Group (speech before the House Democratic Hearing on Corporate Accountability, July 18, 2002). http://democraticleader.house.gov/uploads/020718 corp.accountability.transcript.htm (accessed October 13, 2002).
12. Friedman, 122-26.
13. Jerry Z. Muller, *Adam Smith and His Times* (Princeton, N.J.: Princeton University Press, 1993), 2.
14. Clifton R. Wharton, CEO, TIAA-CREF, "Responsibility in a Common World: My Brother's Keeper?" Vital Speeches of the Day (New York, June 1, 2002). Retrieved from http://proquest.umi.com/pqdweb on September 21, 2002.
15. Matt. 25:21.
16. Michael Hudson, "It Shall Be a Jubilee unto You" *Yes! Magazine* (Fall 2002), 38.
17. Lev. 25:28.
18. Lev. 19:9-10 (NIV).
19. Lev. 25:23-24 (NIV).
20. Milton Friedman, "The Suicidal Impulse of the Business Community" (luncheon address, November 21, 1998), The Annual Cato Institute/Forbes ASAP, Washington, D.C. vx. Silicon Valley Conference on Technology & Society. http://www.cato.org/events/friedman/html (accessed May 28, 2002).
21. Hinkley, 27.
22. Hinkley, 28.
23. As cited in Jill Andresky Fraser, *White-Collar Sweatshop: The Deterioration of Work and Its Rewards in Corporate America* (New York: W. W. Norton & Company), 36.
24. John de Graff, David Wann, and Thomas H. Naylor, *Affluenza: The All-Consuming Epidemic* (San Francisco: Barrett-Koehler Publishers, Inc.), 230.
25. Paul Hawken, *The Ecology of Commerce: A Declaration of Sustainability* (New York: HarperCollins Publishers, 1993), xiii.
26. Friedman (see ch. 4, n. 5), 25.
27. Friedman (see ch. 4, n. 5).

28. Thea Singer, "Can Business Still Save the World?" Inc. (April 1, 2001). http://www.inc.com/articles/growth/entrep_skills/entrep_skills_basics/22319.html (accessed September 25, 2002).
29. Watson Wyatt WorkUSA 2002 Study, as cited by Mike Myers, "Communication Is First Casualty of Recession," Star Tribune, sec. D, September 11, 2002.
30. Patrick Delaney, "Unintended Consequences," Star Tribune, sec. D, October 21, 2002.
31. Transcript of NOW with Bill Moyers, "Risky Business," http://www.pbs.org.now/transcript/transcript_corppanel.html (accessed September 27, 2002).
32. Ezek. 47:8-12 (NIV).
33. Belitsky, "Portrait: Aaron Feuerstein" (see ch. 4, n. 3).
34. http://www.honesttea.com/company/content/html (accessed September 18, 2002).
35. Ibid.
36. Heidi Prescott, "Bethesda, Md.-Based Honest Tea Stays True to Independent Spirit," South Bend Tribune, March 20, 2002.
37. Daniel T. Ostas, "Deconstructing Corporate Social Responsibility: Insights from Legal and Economic Theory," American Business Law Journal 38, no. 2 (2001), 261.
38. Deut. 25:15-16 (NIV).
39. Sandeep A. Patel and George Dallas, "Transparency and Disclosure: Overview of Methodology and Study Results—United States," Standard & Poor's (October 16, 2002).
40. See ch. 4, n. 11.
41. "Built to Flip—Where Do You Come Down?" Fast Company 32 (2000), 144. http://pf.fastcompany.com/online/32/flipdia.html (accessed October 13, 2002).
42. His Holiness the Dalai Lama and Howard C. Cutler, The Art of Happiness (New York: Riverhead Books, 1998), 29.
43. Mark O'Keefe, "For Taxpayers, 'Rich' Is an Ever-Changing Term," Star Tribune, sec. D, January 12, 2003.
44. Ibid.
45. Eccl. 2:26.
46. de Graff, Wann, and Naylor, Affluenza, 24.
47. O'Keefe (see. n. 43 above).
48. Heylar, John. "The Only Company Wal-Mart Fears," Fortune Magazine, November 24, 2003, 158.

Chapter 5

1. Ellen Hickey and Yenyen Chan, "Tobacco and the Huichol Indians," Pesticide Action Network. www.panna.org/resources/documents/tobacco.pdf (accessed January 21, 2003).
2. Anita Roddick, Business As Unusual (London: Thorsons, 2000), 13-14.
3. Isa. 58:6 (NLT).
4. Roddick, Business As Unusual, 29. During the April 2000 protests in Washington, D.C., seventy of the male protestors arrested for such minor charges as parading without a permit were denied contact with their lawyers for up to thirty hours at a time, left handcuffed and shackled, denied food for over thirty hours and water for up to ten. They were assigned public defenders instead of their own lawyers, in violation of legal ethics. Their statement to the public can be found at http://www.globalexchange.org/wbimf/jailedstatement.html.
5. Ruth Rosen, "The Power of Peaceful Protest," San Francisco Chronicle, July 25, 2002. http://www.alternet.org/story.html?StoryID=13677 (accessed September 16, 2002).
6. Based on Ezek. 34:18-24.
7. Annual Stockholder Report, McDonald's Corporation, 2001, 6.
8. Korten, When Corporations Rule the World, 76.
9. Andrew Berg and Anne Krueger, "Lifting All Boats: Why Openness Helps Curb Poverty," Finance & Development 39, no. 3 (2002), 16.
10. Ibid.
11. Phil Stewart, "Columbia Leader Says Trying to Avoid Economic Ruin," Reuters, (September 22, 2002). http://www.forbes.com/newswire/2002/09/22/rtr7277984.html (accessed October 1, 2002).
12. Simon Gardner, "Paraguay Bottlenecked in New Anti-Government Protest," Reuters,

(September 25, 2002). http://www.forbes.co/newswire/2002/09/25/rtr732084.html (accessed October 1, 2002).

13. "US Envoy Sounds Out Brazilian Candidates' Policies," *Reuters* (August 26, 2002). www.forbes.com/newswire/2002/08/26/rtr705206.html (accessed October 1, 2002).

14. Korten, 47.

15. Source: Statistical Abstracts of the United States.

16. Source: Information Please Almanac—1995.

17. Kotter, 147.

18. As quoted in Noam Chomsky, *Profit over People: Neoliberalism and Global Order* (New York: Seven Stories Press, 1998), 52.

19. From the *American Journalism Review* (November 1998), as quoted in Ben H. Bagdikian, *The Media Monopoly,* 6th ed. (Boston: Beacon Press, 2000).

20. By Peter Phillips (Boston: Seven Stories Press, 1991).

21. As quoted in Kotter, 64.

22. Ezek. 34:21-22 (NLT).

23. George Soros, *The Crisis of Global Capitalism* [Open Society Endangered] (New York: PublicAffairs/Perseus Books Group), 1998, xxvii.

24. As quoted in Chomsky, *Profit over People,* 20. Chomsky is a professor of linguistics at Massachusetts Institute of Technology and a political activist.

25. Bruce Horovitz. "Scandals Shake Public; Americans Have Great Faith in Each Other, But Their Trust in CEOs, Big Business, Priests and HMOs Is Slipping Away," *USA Today,* July 16, 2002.

26. Robert Weissman, "Why We Protest," *Washington Post,* Monday, September 10, 2001. http://www.washingtonpost.com/ac2/wp-dyn/A2054-2001sep9? (accessed January 21, 2003).

27. "Promoting Better National Institutions: The Role of the IMF." Panel discussion at the IMF's Third Annual Research Conference, Washington, D.C., November 8, 2002. http://www.imf.org/external/np/tr/2002/tr021108.htm.

28. Excerpt from Joseph Stiglitz, *Globalization and Its Discontents* (New York: W. W. Norton & Company), as reprinted in The Milken Institute Review. http://216.239.39.100/search?q=cache:TE5mApcRuX0C:www.milkeninstitute.org/ review/2002qtr3/pdf/54-73.pdf+%22Joseph+Stiglitz%22+%22research%22 +%22Nobel&hl=en&ie=UTF-8 (accessed January 22, 2003).

29. Joseph E. Stiglitz, *Globalization and Its Discontents,* 206.

30. Benjamin R. Barber, *Jihad vs. McWorld: How Globalism and Tribalism Are Reshaping the World* (New York: Ballantine Books, 1996), 71-72.

31. Robert Weissman, "Why We Protest," *Washington Post,* September 10, 2001. http://www.washingtonpost.com/ac2/wp-dyn/A2054-2001sep9? (accessed January 21, 2003).

32. "Caux Round Table Principles for Business." http://www.cauxroundtable.org/ ENGLISH.HTM (accessed October 29, 2002). The Principles were based on The Minnesota Principles, a statement of business behavior developed by the Minnesota Center for Corporate Responsibility. The Center hosted and chaired the drafting committee, which included representatives from Japan, Europe, and the United States.

33. Ezek. 34:11-12, 20-22.

34. Pam Leigh, "Training's New Guard 2001: Michael Margolis," *Training and Development* 5, no. 5 (2001), 58-59.

35. Roddick, *Business As Unusual,* 170.

36. Roddick, *Business As Unusual,* 242.

37. http://www.hannaandersson.com/Static.asp?pg=11&scid= MBUK4JS6XVSN9HVMKNF7M6JKTVGV2DXA (accessed September 17, 2002).

38. Jerry Useem, "Fortune 500: No. 2—Exxon's African Adventure," *Fortune* 145, no. 5 (2002), 102-14.

39. Editorial, "Development and Poverty," *The Oil and Gas Journal* 100, no. 36 (2002), 17.

40. 1 John 3:17-18.

41. Frances Moore Lappé and Anna Lappé, "Of Land and Hope," *Yes! Magazine* (Fall 2002). http://www.yesmagazine.org/23livingeconomy/lappe.htm (accessed October 1, 2002).

42. 1 Cor. 1:20 (NIV).
43. "Toys of Misery Update: Action Alert!" National Labor Committee. www.nlc.org/china/ (accessed January 6, 2003).
44. From the Web site of Global Exchange, http://www.globalexchange.org/stores/ fairtrade.html, (accessed October 15, 2002).
45. The source for Li Chunmei's story is Philip P. Pan, "Worked Till They Drop: Few Protections for China's New Laborers," *The Washington Post,* May 13, 2002. Retrieved from http://www.sweatshopwatch.org/swatch/headlines/2002/china_may02.html (Accessed January 6, 2003).
46. As quoted in de Graaf Wann, Naylor, *Affluenza,* 61.
47. Second Inaugural Address, January 20, 1937. As quoted in *Bartlett's Familiar Quotations,* 16th ed., Justin Kaplan, gen. ed. (Boston: Little, Brown & Company, Inc., 1992), 649.

Chapter 6

1. Dee Hock, *Birth of the Chaordic Age* (San Francisco: Barrett-Koehler Publishers, Inc., 1999), 24.
2. As quoted in de Graaf, Wann, and Naylor, *Affluenza,* 72.
3. 1 Cor. 12:27 (NIV).
4. 1 Cor. 12:12.
5. 1 Cor. 12: 17-19.
6. Brian O'Reilly, "The New Deal: What Companies and Employees Owe One Another," *Fortune* 129, no. 12 (1994), 44.
7. As quoted in de Graaf, Wann, and Naylor, *Affluenza,* 42.
8. From a survey by International Survey Research Corporation, as referenced in Fraser, *White-Collar Sweatshop,* 30.
9. Ibid.
10. 1 Cor. 12:24-25 (NIV).
11. Shawn Tully, "Why Drug Prices Will Go Lower," *Fortune* (May 13, 1993), as referenced in Hawken, *The Ecology of Commerce,* 127.
12. 1 Cor. 12:26 (NIV).
13. As quoted in de Graaf, Wann, and Naylor, *Affluenza,* 50.
14. Neal St. Anthony, "Doing Right By Its Employees Pays Off for Reell." *Star Tribune,* sec. D, January 25, 2002.
15. Ibid.
16. De Geus, *The Living Company,* 21.
17. Gordon MacKenzie, *Orbiting the Giant Hairball: A Corporate Fool's Guide to Surviving with Grace* (New York: Viking, 1996), 178.
18. Jim Collins, *Good to Great: Why Some Companies Make the Leap . . . and Others Don't* (New York: HarperCollins, 2001), 42.
19. Visit http://www.busineskeys.com for more information.
20. Interview with Fred Rogers by guest host Barbara Bogaev aired on Fresh Air, National Public Radio, November 13, 2002. Coproduced by Terry Gross and Danny Miller. http://www.npr.org/dmg/audioplayer.php?prgCode=FA&showDate= 28-Feb-2003&segNum=3v (accessed March 4, 2003).
21. David Henry, "Mergers: Why Most Big Deals don't Pay Off," *Business Week* (October 14, 2002), 60.
22. http://www.circadian.com.
23. Don Cohen and Laurence Prusak, *In Good Company: How Social Capital Makes Organizations Work* (Boston: Harvard Business School Press, 2001), 4.
24. Robin Dunbar, *Grooming, Gossip, and the Evolution of Language* (Cambridge, Mass.: Harvard University Press, 1996), 206.
25. Hock, *Birth of the Chaordic Age,* 132.
26. Knight Kiplinger, "Patriotic Hiring." Broadcast on Marketplace, September 20, 2001. Produced by J. J. Yore, produced in Los Angeles by Minnesota Public Radio.
27. Hock, *Birth of the Chaordic Age,* 96.

28. Leslie Kaufman, "Some Companies Derail the "Burnout" Track," *New York Times*, sec. A, May 4, 1999. http://web.lexis-nexis.com.
29. "Husky Injection Molding Systems Ltd. Is Profiled; Discusses Downsizings, Going Public in 1998, and Corporate Strategy," *Modern Plastics* 79, no. 1 (2002), 52ff.
30. Peter Block, *Stewardship* (San Francisco: Barrett-Koehler Publishers, Inc., 1993).
31. http://www.containerstore.com/learn/index.jhtml;$sessionid$PQJZAEAAAAK5NQ FIAIKCFE4AVABBIIV0 (accessed February 20, 2003).
32. "Employee Turnover: A Critical Human Resource Benchmark," HR Benchmarks, Employment Policy Foundation, December 3, 2002. http://216.239.57.100/search?q=cache:ewC3oJx9AoEC:www.epf.org/research/ newsletters/2002/hb20021203.pdf+%22employee+turnover+rate%22+%22retail% 22&hl=en&ie=UTF-8.
33. Matthew Fox, *The Reinvention of Work: A New Vision of Livelihood for Our Time* (New York: HarperCollins Publishers, 1994), 103.
34. 1 Cor. 12:21-23 (NIV).
35. Boston: Little, Brown, 1981.
36. D. C. Fontana and Laurence N. Wolfe, "The Ultimate Computer," in *Star Trek*, vol. 9 by James Blish (New York: Bantam Books, 1973), 65.

Chapter 7

1. Kofi Annan, "Address to the World Summit on Sustainable Development," September 2, 2002, Johannesburg (Africa News Service, September 3, 2002). Copyright © 2002 United Nations.
2. Joan Lowy, "Cell phones Linked to Slaughter of Gorillas," *Star Tribune*, sec. A, June 23, 2002.
3. Jeremy Lovell, "Asian Smog Cloud Threatens Millions, Says U.N," *Reuters Limited* (London), August 12, 2002. http://story.news.yahoo.com/news?tmpl=story&u=/ nm/20020812/sc_nm/environment_asia_cloud_dc_3 (accessed August 12, 2002).
4. "The Cost of Coal" (television broadcast), Now With Bill Moyers (New York: Public Broadcasting Service). Transcript retrieved on October 3, 2002 from http://www.pbs.org.now.printable/transcript_coal_print.html.
5. Gen. 1:28 (NIV).
6. Jeffrey Kluger and Andrea Dorfman, "The Challenges We Face," *Time*, August 26, 2002.
7. Katherine Sullivan, "A Glimpse of Home," *Time* 160, no. 9 (2002), A5.
8. From an October 2000 interview, as quoted in de Graaf, Wann, and Naylor, *Affluenza*, 234.
9. Annan, "Address to the World Summit On Sustainable Development."
10. As quoted in Korten, *When Corporations Rule the World*, 83.
11. Hawken, *The Ecology of Commerce*, 12.
12. Anthony Flaccavento, "From the Earth Up," *Yes! Magazine* (Fall 2002). http://www.yesmagazine.org/23livingeconomy/flaccavento.htm (accessed October 1, 2002).
13. Defining Quality, Patagonia, Inc., 1998, 26.
14. Meenakshi Ganguly of New Delhi, "Seeds of Self-Reliance," *Time* 160, no. 9 (August 26, 2002), A34.
15. Welling, "Patagonia: Small World View of Big Business" (see ch. 2, n. 19).
16. Hawken, *Growing a Business*, 56.
17. Roper Starch Worldwide's 1996 "Green Gauge" survey, quoted in Carl Frankel, *In Earth's Company* (Gabriola Island, British Columbia: New Society Publishers, 1998), 140.
18. Jane Goodall, "The Power of One," *Time* 160, no. 9 (August 26, 2002), A62
19. Aaron Bernstein,Michael Arndt, Wendy Zellner, and Peter Coy, "Too Much Corporate Power?" *Business Week* (September 11, 2000), 144-58.
20. Robert Shapiro, former CEO, Monsanto, as quoted in *Business Week* (September 11, 2000).
21. http://www.monsanto.com/monsanto/layout/our_commitments/default.asp (accessed September 21, 2002).
22. Daniel Quinn, *Ishmael* (New York: Bantam/Turner, 1992), 4.
23. Job 38:4-7 (NIV).
24. As quoted in de Graaf, Wann, and Naylor, *Affluenza*, 221.

25. Jim Johnson, "Deep Thinking: Sony Exec Explains Radical E-Waste Solution," *Waste News* 8, no. 2 (2000), 1.

26. Amory Lovins, "Natural Capitalism" (lecture, January 28, 2001). http://www.abc.net.au/rn/talks/bbing/stories/s231834.htm (accessed October 7, 2002).

27. Belinda Luscombe, "Staying Cool Is a Breeze," *Time* (August 26, 2002).

28. Katherine Ellison, "His Market Is a Gas," *Time* (August 26, 2002).

29. Jim Motavalli and Josh Harkinson, "Buying Green: Harnessing Large-Scale Procurement Power," Emagazine.com. http://www.greenbiz.com/news/reviews_third.cfm?newsID =22444 (accessed October 8, 2002).

30. Jennifer Macey, "Environmentalists Say Summit a Huge Letdown." Copyright © Deutsche Welle, September 4, 2002. http://www.dw.world.de (accessed October 8, 2002).

31. Sigurd F. Olson, *Open Horizons* (New York: Alfred A. Knopf, Inc., 1969), 224.

32. Ps. 24:1 (NIV).

33. Jim Motavalli and Josh Harkinson, "Buying Green."

34. Collins, *Good to Great,* 165.

35. Jim Motavalli and Josh Harkinson, "Buying Green."

36. Ibid.

37. Kaplan, J., ed. *Bartlett's Familiar Quoations,* 16th ed. (Boston: Little, Brown, and Company, 1992), 537.

Chapter 8

1. M. Scott Peck, *The Different Drum* (New York: Simon & Schuster, 1987), 184-85.

2. Matt. 25:13 (NIV).

3. Hock, *Birth of the Chaordic Age,* 311.